ACT AND BEING

Dietrich Bonhoeffer

ACT AND BEING

Translated by
Bernard Noble

Introduction by
Ernst Wolf

HARPER & ROW, PUBLISHERS

New York and Evanston

This book under the title of
AKT UND SEIN
was first published in 1956 by
Christian Kaiser Verlag, Munich

Act and Being, Bonhoeffer's inaugural dissertation of 1931, develops the questions raised in *Sanctorum Communio* in the direction of the problem of " being in the truth." At the same time and in face of the real or apparent theological fronts just prior to the beginning of the church struggle, Bonhoeffer is attempting a genuine " mediation." He traces these fronts back to the encounter of a theology of " act " (contingency, discontinuity, transcendentalism, reference to existence, and decision) with a theology of " being " (givenness, continuity, metaphyous objectification, and " doctrine ") and, by analogy, to the corresponding confrontation between cardinal, mutually exclusive philosophical positions: Transcendentalism (Kant) and Ontology (Heidegger). The vain struggle for truth in the sphere of an autonomous self-understanding of man, presented in the first part of this book, is taken with its problems on to the level of the church as " the occurrence of truth " and set forth anew as a problem within the reality of revelation. The solution of the problem of " act " versus " being " is reached in terms of revelation and the church, and, in the concept of revelation itself, is understood within the community of persons, over against the one-sided " act " interpretation (whether theocentric, as with Barth, or anthropocentric, as with Bultmann) or the equally one-sided " being " interpretation with its doctrine of the self-binding of the freedom of God. Bonhoeffer attempts to comprehend the continuity of the new being in faith with the human-personal ego as a whole in the reality of the community. The dialectic of *simul justus et peccator* is here met with as the dialectic of " being in Adam," i.e. " in untruth," and " being in Christ," i.e. " in truth."

Just as *Sanctorum Communio* dealt with the dogmatic comprehension of the church by uniting sociological and theological categories, so here dogmatics is grounded in the reality of the church, in " Christ existing as community." The notion that theology is a function of the church is taken up with great care—not wholly clear in the philosophical introduction but illuminating in the second part, the dogmatic examination—such that the church, the " place where being is comprehended," is presented as the unity of act and being.

With his considerations and attempts at a solution of this problem, Bonhoeffer's work may be set alongside questions which to-day have become so pressing concerning the nature of theology as such: the tension between theological existentialism and neo-orthodox " pure doctrine," and " self-understanding " of Christian being in the world over against its dissolution in religiosity.

Göttingen, June 1956

ERNST WOLF

6

CONTENTS

Contents

The Problem

It seems to me that the latest developments in theology can be interpreted as an attempt to come to grips with the problem of act and being. Karl Barth, with his "critical reservation", wishes to maintain the freedom of God's grace, and to establish human existence on that ground; Friedrich Gogarten and Rudolf Bultmann seek to remove man from his own disposal in the "concrete situation", "historicality"; H. M. Müller pins decision, in the contingency of temptation, to the "*propter Christum*"; F. K. Schumann, blaming idealist epistemology for the ruin of theology up to and including Barth, has gone in quest of an objective idea of God. On the other side, Paul Althaus is anxious to salvage a theology of faith from the wreck of that of consciousness, while Emmanuel Hirsch, in the line of R. Seeberg's and Karl Holl's Lutheran studies, seeks the Christian's "being" in consciousness *qua* conscience, *qua* new will. · Brunstäd unites man and God in the "unconditional personality". E. Peterson has discovered in pure phenomenology an arm against dialectical theology and sees in theological concepts pure essential and ontological abstractions. Two philosophical viewpoints, Heidegger's onto-phenomenological analysis of existence *qua existentia* and Grisebach's virtual counter-thesis, his "critical philosophy" of the contingent present, have found a hearing in theology. Finally, the Catholic and Thomist E. Przywara, who assesses the theological position of both camps with marvellous clarity, puts forward his ontology of the *analogia entis* in opposition to dialectical theology's pre-occupation with the act. All these viewpoints illustrate at bottom a widespread wrestling with the same problem, one which is theology's legacy from Kant and idealism. The problem is one of forming genuine theological concepts and of choosing whether one is to use ontological categories in explaining them or those of transcendental philosophy. It is a question of the " objectivity " of the concept God, of an adequate concept of knowledge, of defining the relation between the " being of God " and the mental act which conceives it. In other words, there has to be a theological interpretation of what " the being of God in revelation " means and how it is known, of what may be the interrelation of belief as act and revelation as being, and correspondingly of where man stands when seen from the standpoint of revelation. Is revelation merely what is " given " to man in the per-formance of a certain act, or is there such a thing for him in revelation as a " being "? What form is taken by the concept of revelation if we explain it in terms of the act, and what other form if in terms of a " being "?

Here it is not our intention to apply the dichotomy of act and being as a critical principle to the history of theology, not even the most recent, though our inquiry can scarcely avoid touching upon matters of present concern, but to demonstrate in systematic outline the significance of the act-being problem for dogmatics as a whole.

The juxtaposition of act and being is not identical with that of consciousness and being, for the latter pair of concepts is not mutually exclusive in its terms. Even consciousness has predicates of being, for as conscious-*ness* it embodies the ontological category of the conscious. The act, inasmuch as it is pure intentionality, must be considered wholly alien to being. That it is consciously executed necessitates the distinction between direct (*actus directus*) and reflexive (*actus reflexus*) consciousness: in the first, consciousness is simply " directed at "; in the second, it can become objectively conscious of itself in reflexion. It is not, then, that the act offers no *material* to reflexion, only that the intentionality of the direct act is automatically displaced by reflexion—in relation to which, therefore, it cannot stand as a datum that was " there " for the finding. Later this distinction will prove to have decisive importance in theology.

Even as conscious*ness*, being is not contained within *conscious*ness. As something taking place in consciousness, the act is a temporal psychic phenomenon, but it is not really understood by being " explained " as an event in time, no more is " being " understood through definition as " entity " (or even, say, conscious entity [1]). The act, as Dilthey said, can never be " explained " but only " understood ", just as being can never be " proved " but only " shown ". It follows that we are here concerned with realities transcending " the entity ". All hopes for a genuine ontology or transcendental philosophy must come to grief if this is not understood.

At this point let us lay down a few quite general and preliminary definitions about the nature of act and being, from which we can proceed in our inquiry. If outward reference, infinite extensity, restriction to the conscious,

[1] *Bewusst-Seiendes.*

existentiality [1] and discontinuity are comprised in the act, being comprises a strict self-confinement, infinite *in*-tensity, transcendence of the conscious, and continuity. How a concrete understanding of both is reached in philosophy and theology remains to be seen. But it must already be obvious that the whole of theology, in its theory of the knowledge of God, of man, of sin and grace, crucially depends on whether it elects to stress concepts of act or of being at the outset.

It is intended to examine the problem systematically, stage by stage, as follows:

The problem of knowledge offers the first context in which light is shed on the problem of act and being. When we come to the concept of the object it becomes an acute necessity to explain in terms of the act or of being; if we resolve that concept wholly in terms of the act-subject, this must produce intolerable consequences for any science insisting on the indispensability of objective ontological concepts—and vice versa. For the question of knowledge is the self questioning the self, the self-testing of understanding of existence, the I's reflexive self-placing into a world, or wanting to find itself in a world: it is the question of man. Though one does not follow from the other, the connection is there in the nature of things: the meaning of epistemology is anthropology. It is because man himself, no less, is at stake that the passion for philosophising has flared into life whenever, since Descartes, man's capacity to know has been in dispute. But inasmuch as the necessity for the knowing to transcend the known, or vice versa, is comprised in the

[1] Here " existentiality " does not designate the sphere of " there is ", but the person's central, potential involvement.

14

very concept of knowledge, the understanding of existence in relation to transcendence is part and parcel of the problem of knowledge in all its forms, which implies that the problem of God, in some way, also comes into question. This is even true (as we mean to show) when one tries to exclude completely the question of God, or when, as in Heidegger's ontology, epistemology is allotted quite another place in the totality of philosophy than transcendentalism allows. It is true because the question of man lies hidden in epistemology, whether the transcendental attempt is being made to explain in terms of the act-subject, or the ontological attempt to explain in purely objective terms of " being ". (For these two represent the most sharply antithetic formulations of any given position in epistemology.)

It follows that the critical idea which must govern the argument of Part One, below, is the possibility of applying suggested solutions of the act-being problem to the Christian ideas of God and revelation, on which all further theory is conditional. The test of this possibility will be provided by the underlying self-understanding of men asserted in any given case. For even if we can envisage the applicability of the purely transcendental or ontological theses to other fields of inquiry, the possibility of constructing a genuine theology on one or other concept of knowledge founders on the attendant human self-understanding, which we discover to be that of an autonomous I understanding itself and in its own power. In principle, the idea of a contingent revelation of God in Christ denies the possibility of the I's self-comprehension outside the reference to revelation (Christian transcendentalism). The idea of revelation must therefore yield an epistemology of its own. But inasmuch as analysis of revelation in terms whether of a cort being [1] produces concepts of knowledge unsuited to bear the whole weight of revelation, the idea of revelation must be re-envisaged within the concretion of the idea of the Church, i.e. in a sociological category where both kinds of analysis encounter each other and are drawn together in one.[2] The dialectic of act and being is here recognisable in theological terms as the dialectic of faith and the communion of Christ; neither is to be imagined without the other, but each is " suspended " in the other. The theological concepts of knowledge and object are shown to be determined by the sociological category of the person and must reshape themselves accordingly. The sphere of the entity, of " there is ," of frozen ontological concepts, is thawed into motion by the sociological category. Concepts of being, inasmuch as deriving from revelation, are always determined by the concepts of sin and grace, " Adam " and Christ. In theology there are no pre-existing categories of pure creature-hood which are divorced from these concepts. The idea of this " being "—of sin and man in sin, of grace and man in grace—is in Part Three developed within the wider concretion of the idea of the Church. Our investigation ends with an analysis of " being in Christ " as determined by past and future, reflexion and intentionality. The past is " suspended " in the future, reflexion in intentionality. Out of the man of conscience is formed the child.

The whole represents an attempt to unify the aims of true transcendentalism and true ontology within an " ecclesiastical thought ".

[1] Part Two, Chapters 1 and 2.
[2] Part Two, Chapter 3.

PART ONE

The problem of act and being, treated as the epistemological problem in philosophy's understanding of Dasein

I

THE TRANSCENDENTAL ENDEAVOUR

Epistemology is the self's attempt to understand itself. I reflect on myself, and I and my-self separate, then they fuse again: that is the basic attitude of the transcendental philosopher, and somehow or other the I's self-understanding is comprised in this attitude of reflexion. In regarding itself the intention of the I is self-understanding. Here we see the common germinal cell of transcendental philosophy and idealism.

In what follows, two considerations must be kept in view. Firstly, we must distinguish between genuine transcendental philosophy, the concept which Kant endeavoured to amplify from its long evolution reaching back farther than scholastic theology,[1] and the concept of transcendentalist philosophy as understood by post-Kantian idealism.[2] Secondly, we must bear in mind the question whether Kant's transcen-

---

[1] Cf. H. Knittermeyer, " Die Transzendentalphilosophie und die Theologie," *Christliche Welt,* 1924, especially p. 222.

[2] All that follows below by way of representing Kantian or idealist philosophy is stylised (and therefore dispenses with quotations). Kant is represented as a pure transcendental philosopher, which he never was entirely, though we believe he intended to be one. It is the system we debate, not matters of historical fact.

dental critique of reason is altogether identical with the criticism of reason in Luther and orthodox Protestant dogmatics; we must ask whether Kant was not, rather, bent on using delimitation to establish reason in its rights: if this were so it would be impermissible to claim him as the representative epistemologist of Protestantism.[1]

To the concept of genuine transcendentalism belongs the reference of thought to something transcendental, but not its having that something at its disposal. All thinking has a double reference to the transcendental: a *retrospective*, inasmuch as it claims, *qua* thought, a meaning which it cannot give to itself, and inasmuch as meaning is connected with the logos of the transcendental, and also a *prospective* reference to objects within which, supposing they are truly *ob*jective (conceive " object " how you will—with Kant, with Rickert or no matter who), something transcending thought stands over against it. So long as the resistance of transcendence to thought is asserted, i.e. so long as the thing-in-itself and transcendental apperception are understood as irreducible definitive concepts, neither of which is involved in the other, we may speak of genuine transcendentalism:—

In knowing, human existence is aware of itself as in tension between two poles which transcend it, and this " being amid " transcendence is *Dasein*. [2] But this acquires another, special meaning through thought. All entity among which human *Dasein* is situated " has reference to " human

[1] Cf. W. Lütgert's interpretation in *Die Religion des Idealismus*, I, pp. 8ff.

[2] The concept of *Dasein* as the mode of being peculiar to man as distinct from other forms of being is here taken over from Heidegger's *Sein und Zeit*, 1927.

Dasein by virtue of thought, that same thought which permits *Dasein* to be understood as being between poles of transcendence, or which understands itself to be so placed. In this way human *Dasein* acquires a mode of being which sets it apart from all other entity. In human *Dasein* the world of other entity is transcended; indeed, it exists only in reference to thought—though whether, also, only *by* thought is another question—and the ontological category of human *Dasein*, which has these remarkable characteristics, is for genuine transcendentalism the *act* pure and simple. That is the astounding, but necessary, consequence. "Being" is being between transcendent poles, but that is only on account of the will to self-understanding which is reference to transcendence. The knowing oneself to refer to the transcendental, but to be also, for that reason, the world's point of reference, that, for transcendentalism, is human existence.

It is from this delimitation and restriction of self-understanding man, i.e. of reason, that the radical critique of reason springs. Yet inasmuch as reason itself becomes the critic of reason, it is reinstated in its original rights; in other words, man understands himself in the last resort not from the transcendental but from himself, from reason or from the bounds which reason has prescribed to itself, be they ethical or rational in kind. Every transcendental epistemology or corresponding interpretation of existence must peter out in this internal contradiction, and this hiatus, which has its roots deep in the nature of the case, must be taken more seriously than hastily ensuing attempts to restore inner unity, which proceed at the expense of the transcendental premises themselves.

The immediate point which we have to note and examine is this: man is existence as pure act, understanding itself from out its self-imposed bounds, i.e. from itself. Transcendentalism is not phenomenalism. Even if we encounter certain ideas in Kant that have a strongly phenomenalistic ring, it is clear from the question which divides him from phenomenalism that they are foreign to his design. Phenomenalism asked: how does the I come upon the object? and resolved the question by the pure phenomenality of objects in the consciousness. Kant accepts the given relation of I to object and goes on to ask: How is knowledge possible at all, i.e. what is the meaning of this given relationship? Thereby his question differs from the phenomenalistic as a question about a given relation differs from an ontological question. For questions of being are unknown to genuine transcendentalism, and it must be so, since its very sense and purpose is to transcend the " dogmatism " of ontology. Knowing cannot possibly be a simple reflection or copy of reality (if that were so, there would be no criteria of truth), but is possible only by virtue of a synthesis originally founded in the cognitive subject in the unity of transcendental apperception, and there taking place, which must be regarded as having logical precedence over the empirical, over experience—in other words, as a priori. But this synthesis must be internally necessary and regular; therein it gives proof of its truth and validity. It is not through some kind of coincidence with the object of knowledge that knowledge is valid, but through the necessity of the a priori synthesis. Truth is only in the pure act. Thus the concept of being is resolved into the concept of the act. Being " is " only " with reference to " knowing. This " with-reference-to " characterising the original form of transcendentalism still leaves room for thought's essential reference back to the transcendental, whereas any substituted " by virtue of " or " through " would imply the omnipotence of reason over transcendence. Consequently, to understand existence is, for Kant, to know oneself in being as " having reference ", to feel the *radical* challenge which knowledge throws down to the knowing self,[1] to be unable to rest in oneself without surrendering oneself, to be purely and simply the act. But as such the understanding of existence must always be transcendent of itself.[2] It is aimed at itself in a permanent reference, *without any possibility of attaining itself,* for if it were to attain itself it would no longer be " with reference to ", no longer the act and nothing but the act. The endeavour to understand oneself purely from oneself is bound to miscarry, because it is the nature of existence to be not self-contained but simply " with reference to ". However, the very attainment is a logical impossibility, for supposing I knew myself, " myself " would represent a thing completed and attained, but it would no longer be " I " or the attaining act or " with reference to "; " I ", regarded as the attaining act, has yet to become the thing completed and attained. " I " is something which cannot be thought, because it is the precondition at the back of thinking; that is to say, at all times it is already " there " as the a priori synthesis before the object, whose role it can never assume. Now here stands revealed a profound contradiction: As " what

[1] Knittermeyer, in *Zwischen den Zeiten,* 1929, No. 4, pp. 352ff.

[2] Concerning what follows it is necessary to reiterate that this is only one side of the historical Kant, but that ever since Fichte fresh attempts have had to be made to understand Kant better than he understood himself.

is always already there ", as the very act of thinking and its intrinsic precondition, the I logically *precedes* thought. But inasmuch as everything determinable about the I is imbued with the character of noesis, *thought precedes the I.* This means that thought lies on the brink of the " non-objective " without which, since it is the condition of the conditional, there is nothing objective. Thought is the frontier of the general existence out of which man lives, in the sense that the unconditional (the background of existence) is always there for man " already ", but has always " just " slipped past whenever human existence is bent, in thought, on the understanding of existence. From the outset we are thus confronted with the impossibility that human existence should understand itself in its capacity as performance of acts, for the very reason that its essence is the spontaneous performance of acts.

When one is in this way brought up against the barrier in concepts of the I and thought, it is possible to adopt one of two attitudes. By exercising and testing itself against the I, thought suspends itself, but in restricting itself by this self-suspension (and in consequently contrasting with the objective the I in its role of thought's precondition), thought reasserts itself as the only thing which makes such a severance possible. Now thought can bow to this self-limitation, in the manner of genuine transcendentalism, and this attitude seems to me to accord with Kant's original design, though in the historical Kant it is admittedly inextricable (in a way which invites misunderstanding) from phenomenalistic and idealistic elements.

Alternatively—and this is philosophy's great temptation —thought can promote itself to be lord and master of the non-objective, in that it takes the doing and thinking I into itself and makes the self-thinking I no longer the *ne plus ultra* of philosophy but its point of *departure*. It cannot do this, however, without losing two things: reality and transcendence, or *one by the other*. Philosophy, thought, the I, are forfeit to themselves instead of to the transcendental. Hence the immensity of thought's claim is transformed into the opposite; thought languishes in itself, for where there is freedom from the transcendental, from reality, there is imprisonment in the self. From the original transcendental thesis has evolved a system characterised by thought's sheer self-transcendentalisation or (which comes to the same thing) a monism unadulterated with reality; whether it is styled a system of pure transcendence or pure immanence, the end-product is materially the same. Kierkegaard said, justly enough, that philosophising of this kind patently forgets that one exists. This second possibility was grasped and elaborated as much in the transition from Socrates to Plato, though of course in quite a different way, as pre-eminently in that from Kant to idealism. It alone holds the key and permit of the system: therein lies its mysterious power.

Whether thought demeans itself modestly, i.e. remains genuine transcendental thinking, or misappropriates the unconditional and becomes idealistic thinking, that is no longer a question of theoretical philosophy (which simply provides, as shown, a choice of two possibilities) but a decision of practical reason. There is nothing to oblige thought, as free thinking, not to annex the unconditional or empower itself of its I. Yet it is no less an act of free thought if, in order to remain free, it contents itself with reference to transcendence and—for the same reason, that it is only relative, referential—refrains from taking over its I. Here at the apogee of thought, though not merely to justify any stinting of hard cogitation, there comes to the fore that decision-character which thought assumes once it is no longer subject to a compulsion of internal logic [1]; it is this that Fichte expresses in his dictum that the kind of philosophy a man has depends on the sort of man he is.[2]

Inasmuch as idealism deprives self-understanding existence of its transcendental reference, i.e. delivers it from the clamping embrace of being between transcendent poles, it seems to have resolved the concept of being, which in pure transcendentalism still appeared to adhere to the transcendental in some possible way, entirely into the concept of the act. It has drawn out Kant's findings to the radical extreme. To *be* is to be comprehended by the I in the a priori synthesis.[3] Without I there is no being; I is creative, the sole efficient; I goes out from itself, and to itself returns. A being which was not the potential object of understanding, but was absolutely thought-projected, would lead directly to materialism. Idealism is neighbour to materialism, Hegel to Marx. Existence, then, is the in-turning, returning or homecoming of the eternal I to itself; this, understood as the eternal act, is self-understanding from the self, for whence could come any self-understanding from

[1] The issue can be decided in a third way, by pure ontology. On this point more is said below.

[2] *Werke*, I, p. 434.

[3] In this connection cf. Brunstäd's *Idee der Religion*, 1922. As this writer sees it, Kant and idealism are contiguous; in his exposition of idealism he traces with exemplary clarity the development in idealistic interpretation of the basic theme—the a priori synthesis.

outside the self if the I is the creator of its world? Mind is understood from mind; thus I can understand myself from myself, or one might add " from God ": insofar as God is in me, God is the unconditional personality which I am.[1] In this process all ontological concepts appear to have fallen by the wayside, and a refined concept of the act rules both epistemology and anthropology. Yet with this apparent radicalisation of the transcendental position something surprising has come to pass. If in original transcendentalism the mind of man was in tension between transcendent poles and was thus irrevocably their co-ordinate, henceforth the movement of the mind is purely self-illumined,[2] which is to say that in principle it has come to rest. The mind's forth-proceeding from itself ensues only under the conditions of its being by itself; hence in this movement the mind remains always in full possession of itself, it can never get into the embarrassing position of merely " being in reference to " the transcendental. Nevertheless, mind residing in itself, even if in a (dialectically unreal) movement, is " substance ", i.e. absolute being, so that Hegel could well say that the one thing he felt obliged to hold against Spinoza was his failing to define substance itself as subjectivity.[3] In fact idealism, especially in Hegel, appears to achieve a synopsis of act and being which would be capable of satisfying the demands of the problem—if only the philosopher's reasoning did not founder on the resistance of his own reality. Hegel wrote a philosophy of angels, but not of human existence.

[1] Cf. Brunstäd's idea of the unconditional personality, in which God and I are one.

[2] Luther, *Röm. Komm.* II, 136, 28, ed. Ficker: *ratio in se ipsam incurva.*

[3] *Werke*, 15, 409, quoted in Hirsch, *Die idealistische Philosophie und das Christentum*, 1926, p. 61, n. 4.

It simply is not true that concrete man (including even the philosopher) is in full possession of the mind. Whoever countenances the idea that he need only arrive at himself to be in God is doomed to hideous disillusion in experiencing the utter introversion, the treadmill confinement to the self, of the very loneliest solitude, with its tormenting desolation and sterility. Concrete man sees himself placed in a contingent here-or-there as one who has to find his whereabouts by asking, thinking and doing, one who has to relate to himself the position pre-given to him and at the same time define himself " with reference to " it. And the imposition, the outrage, which man feels at " being already " " with reference to " some other thing which transcends him—is something essentially different from a certainty of bearing within himself the possibility of mastering the world. In sum, even the *character* of the act, what it means to be an agent, is more purely expressed in the genuine transcendental understanding of existence than in idealism's conflation of act and being. Only when existence, supposed in permanent orientation to transcendence, is said not to be able to understand itself (or only to understand that it does not understand itself) is the true sense of *the act* expressed: act as an ever-shifting " with reference to ", as utter intentionality, as something which gives proof of itself in the psychic process but is only to be understood on the far side of it, act as " direct " consciousness—*actus directus*. Here philosophising itself has an essential connection with existence, and this can be so because it places itself within the responsibility of human existence and frames questions only from out that context; accordingly the question itself is proper to existence and does not involve the answer before-

28

hand. Thus philosophising partakes of the act-character of existence and does not make statements from the standpoint of an existing stock of property such as might inhere in a "being".

Idealism, of course, also seems to perpetuate the transcendental thesis in allowing the reality of the external world to be understood only from the starting-point of the I. Kant's a priori synthesis and Fichte's intellectual intuition (*Anschauung*) seem identical in respect of founding the external world's reality in the I; yet even here genuine transcendentalism must come to a more modest conclusion than idealism: the former judges there is no knowledge capable of passing beyond the proposition that phenomena (the external world) "refer to" the I and are therefore knowable only via the I. It does not lie within the competence of purely transcendental thought to proceed therefrom to a negative or positive judgment as to the being of the phenomenal world. Idealism, however, feels impelled to add the finishing touch by replacing the transcendental reference with an ontological judgment entailing the creative power of the I, and so it comes to distort the meaning of transcendentalism by radicalisation. Now it is no mere chance that idealism, which begins with an ontological judgment, finishes, as shown, with something very like a new concept of substance, so that the pure concept of the act is left to transcendentalism. The world, i.e. the objects of my knowledge, " has reference to me "—that is the transcendental judgment; but idealism pronounces: the world is in being " through me ". This is a distinction which should not be disregarded in the study of systems merely because it remains blurred in the history of philosophy.

On the contrary, it is not hard to see its importance even for theology, as well as for the philosophical theory of God at a given time. The reason why Fichte was unable to make use of Kant in the conflict over atheism derives from the fact that, at bottom, Kant understood himself even better than Fichte thought himself able to understand him. If the world owes its being to the I, there is an exchange of roles between the I and the creator-god; God can no longer become the object of knowledge, but, since he cannot imaginably be the creature of the I, is somehow integrated with the I itself. Thereupon God " is " only in so far as I think, i.e. enter myself in thought.

Transcendentalism proper is dissociated from this attitude by its refusal to turn the I into the Creator, regarding it only as something to which the world must be thought to have reference. In this way there is at least in principle (i.e. so far as this is at all possible in philosophy [1]) no violation of the all-important frontier of creatorhood. Admittedly, here too it is impossible for God to become the object of cognition, otherwise he would have to be thought of as referring to the I (in the way of mundane phenomena) and consequently as essentially existing-for-the-I. By transcendental premises the objectivity of God is an impossibility, since of course all being is understood as entity, as " there is " in a priori synthesis, i.e. is translated into act, and absolute being becomes an idea which is unattainable because it is, as such, wholly non-objective. Thus the concept of God never forsakes the realm of the non-objective, where he abides as the foundation for the possibility of existence

---

[1] Doubtless an oblique reference to the hubris of philosophy, which for Bonhoeffer is *per se* systematic: see pp. 58 and 70 below (*Translator*).

and thought. Transcendental thought can never say " God is "—that would be objectivising, " finitising ", " dogmatising ". Truth " is " only in the act itself, with its reference to transcendence. Only in the action of the act, in existence seeking to understand itself, " is " God—as condition, potentiality—but always in the doing, never in the result. Thus in whatever direction man may turn, God is always at his back.

There is no denying the closeness of God and I in this system. But both remain marginal concepts to which thought and existence simply have permanent " reference ". Yet since transcendentalism is here growing noticeably unsure in its theory, one can scarcely refrain from asking it one further question: what in fact is this " transcendental " to which everything is supposed to refer? If it can never be objectively knowable, how can reason determine its own limits against this unknown? Even if it is to exercise a free decision of practical reason, the outcome is nevertheless reason's self-chosen self-limitation, whereby it reinstates its own authority—as the reason which performed this very limitation. This inmost obscurity in the Kantian concept of the transcendental leads to the discovery that even here, despite the strenuous attempt to surpass itself or prescribe its own limitations, reason is left alone with itself and so understands itself not " with reference to " that which transcends it but with back-reference to itself. The miscarriage of this endeavour to ascertain the bounds of reason is due to the fact that essentially reason *has no* bounds, for in principle the very bound can be thought away until it is no more a genuine boundary. Reason can only be taken into obedience, whether the obedience of speculation, the obedience of *Christ*, or however else. There are bounds only to concrete man as a whole, and their name is Christ.

It only remains to state that in both Kantian transcendentalism and idealism reason is entangled in itself. In these circumstances, " to understand oneself " can only mean " to understand oneself from oneself ", " I am " means " I think " (*cogito—sum*). " God is " means " the mind comes to itself, knows in the unity of consciousness ". In this way the ground seems to crumble under any proposition of genuine belief in God; that is, there is no possibility of asserting the being of God outside the I, since there is only reason alone with itself. At this point it is evident that the I does not advance via itself to any position beyond itself. It is caught up in itself, seeing only itself even when it sees something else, even when it means to see God. It understands itself from itself, to be sure, but this really means that, at bottom, it does not understand itself at all, for it cannot be said to do so until this I feels the overwhelming impact of another I on its existence.[1] It believes itself free and is captive, is overlord of all—yet is itself its only vassal: that is what Protestant dogmatists mean by the corruption of reason. It is ontic narcissism, the *cor curvum* ˄ *se* [2]: if Kant had some inkling of how this would be manifest even, for example, in his doctrine of radical evil, but nevertheless

[1] Bonhoeffer's words could be construed to mean that, in principle, understanding can take place only between an I-subject and an I-object, and that these cannot be entirely identical (because, e.g. of the incompossibility of reflexion and *actus directus*). This indeed is the epistemological aspect of the book's theme. But the author's thought is more radical than epistemology, it is existential and Christian. (*Translator*).

[2] Luther, *Röm. Komm.* II, 137, 1, ed. Ficker.

wrestled—in vain—to overcome the problem by means of the original transcendental thesis, idealism, taking over from Kant, allowed the I to celebrate on this very ground the triumph of its liberation.

Everything now converges on the all-important question which must be put to transcendentalism and idealism alike: *can* the I understand itself from itself? Or is there a fundamental objection?

To " understand " (as distinct from " explain ") is a term whose field of application is represented by states of affairs with a basis of intention, and it comprises the direct consciousness of self-evidence. This latter is only possible in the presence of potential productivity in the direction of the thing to be understood, be it a piece of conduct, an idea or an artistic composition. To understand implies being somehow creative, irrespective of the presence or absence of actual technical ability. In the present case the object to be understood is existence itself, i.e. as an integral whole, for there is no understanding save in a context of unity. If existence is so constructed that the very will to self-understanding belongs to its essence, the problem arises of how the unity of existence can be attained by self-understanding from out the self. The eye does not see itself. It follows that self-understanding existence must be able to think of itself as entire creator of itself (including its self-understanding), and even as creator of its own existence, into which it has been thrust as a self-understander or -nonunderstander; this is self-contradictory from the fact that the " I " must already exist in order to create. Faced with this position the idealistic reason-I [1] nevertheless persists in

---

[1] And in final analysis Kant's transcendental I as well.

33

declaring itself the ultimate entity—" I am what I am " (ontologically meaningful only in application to the concept of God)—in making itself, by an irreducible paradox, its own creator. Alternatively man grasps that this his existentiality, in all its psychophysical ambiguity, is a " being between ", a being " in reference to " something to which existence is a still uncomprehended pointer. In this case, of course, no real understanding of existence is signified, for the self-understanding involved merely characterises the final position attainable by human thought and self-possession. This line of thought can do no more than unfold a new problem of act and being.

In order to solve the problem of thought and being, neo-Kantianism has tried to develop the transcendental thesis on fresh lines. Yet merely by beginning with the thing-in-itself it expresses an ontological instead of a relational judgment, and enters upon the path of Fichte, in making thought the foundation of being. It is a moot point how, say, Cohen's concept of method, derived from transcendentalism, connects with Fichte's quasi-substantial concept of creative mind.[1] While at the outset Natorp here accompanies Cohen, later, in a fresh attempt to master the problem of being, he forms the idea of a " universal logic." [2] The logos lies on the far side of thought and being as that whereby both are possible. Neither is reducible to or suspensible in the other, yet thought is " onto-thinking " and being is " noeto-being ". Quite obviously this speculation, as

[1] Cf. H. Cohen, *System der Philosophie*, I, Logik der reinen Erkenntnis, 1902.

[2] Cf. especially Natorp's latest work, *Praktische Philosophie*, 1925, pp. 1–27.

evidenced by the amalgamation of act and being, has taken us into the Hegel country.

What, in sum, results for the problem of act and being from the transcendental and idealist endeavours? Common to both is the attempt to " raise substance to the subject ",[1] as most thoroughly executed in Hegel's logic: the understanding of the object as an apriori synthesis in transcendental apperception. Thereby being becomes the knowing consciousness. But, as it stands, this proposition is by no means unequivocal. Its positive and its negative interpretations lead in utterly different directions. The thesis that being is given in the cognitive consciousness is certainly not identical with the converse, that in the absence of the cognitive consciousness there is no being. The difference we have noted here comes to the fore: in the positive interpretation the inter-reference of consciousness and transcendent being receives expression; in the negative, the resolution of the latter into the former. But of course the pressing interest of both interpretations is centred on the attention drawn to the mental act of the person. There is no person save in consciousness. In his phenomenology Hegel represented the I's gradual development towards becoming truly a person—a goal attainable only, in the last resort, by philosophical thinking. If anything is to make itself known to me as being, it must be apprehensible by the thinking mind, accordingly the person is only grasped when logical material is under consideration; that is to say, the existence of the person is reached through " meaning ". It follows that the " word " must be allotted an exceptional position, as the only sensible means of communicating

[1] Windelband, *Geschichte der neueren Philosophie*, p. 337.

35

logical material. The person abides in freedom. Knowing takes place in freedom; only in freedom can man's existence grasp and interpret itself. The act, meaning and freedom belong together. Thus the essence of the person is freedom, autonomy, coming-to-itself or being-by-itself.

If at this point they are at one, transcendentalism and idealism part company when they come to express the character of the act. Transcendentalism succeeds in preserving the purity of the act by regarding existence as merely " referring " to something transcendent, but since this transcendent cannot, in Kant, prove itself genuinely transcendent, his version—the original—comes to grief; hence it is that idealism draws the transcendent into itself, and unites act and being within itself, with all the consequences that follow for anthropology. We may see from this that neither in the Kantian orientation to transcendence, nor in idealism's permeation with transcendence, can concepts of being be dispensed with. Yet such an outcome is at variance with the original intention of both.[1]

Now, if theology seeks to espouse this transcendentalist-idealist epistemology, it needs must forfeit a certain right. (Transcendentalist, as distinct from transcendental, is the term with which we shall denote that transcendental philosophy which develops the transcendental thesis into a system

[1] In the history of philosophy one could discover a parallel to nominalism in this attempt to resolve concepts of being. There is no absolute being, not even of concepts: these " are " only in the act of abstraction. But, admittedly, if (as especially in Roscellin de Compiègne) the isolated reality of individual things is excluded from this, we have an interpretation quite alien to idealistic philosophy. For idealism, of course, individual things are only objects of cognition through application of the universal thought-forms and concepts.

of reason.) The *raison d'être* of transcendentalist-idealist epistemology is its claim to involve understanding of existence, hence finally of world and God. Unmindful of that claim, it would abandon its title to consideration. Epistemology is the mind turning to the mind. In the unity of the mind, overriding the subject-object bifurcation, was discovered the fulcrum of the understanding of existence, world and God. If a theology wished to style itself trans-cendentalist-idealist, it would have to accommodate this claim. This is a consideration which severely restricts its own concept of knowledge. Furthermore, the theology would have to translate all being into consciousness. The object, reality, is now an a priori synthesis. A judgment is no longer true as a judgment about a reality transcending consciousness, but true in the " unconditional unity-of-experience of the personality ". [1] This must apply also to statements about God. Correspondingly, as already shown, such a theology can envisage no objective concept of God, since of course the object " is " only in the transcendental unity of apperception, therefore God himself " is ", as in this unity, never imaginable but only operating in the activity of the conscious mind. And so the identity of my non-objective I with God is expressed in what is called the " unconditional personality ".[2] Theology is confronted with the dilemma of either making the objective God the content of consciousness and object of the I-subject, or of

[1] Brunstäd, *op. cit.*, p. 154.

[2] Brunstäd, *op. cit.*, p. 217: the *revelatio specialis* is the disclosure of the unconditional-synthetic personality *as* such, it is the self's comprehension in God as this unconditional personality, " the foundation, effected in God, of the oneness of God's consciousness with self-consciousness ".

permitting the I to locate God in its non-objective I-hood, in its coming to itself.

God " is " not, outside the conscious mind coming to itself. " The ultimate, true reality is that which is attested in our self-activity, our I-hood." [1] Once non-objectivity, then, is taken seriously, God is never but in the act of the self-knowing mind. Even as a component of philosophising, God is not an objective entity, but is only in the execution of the philosophising act. But while the process of genuine transcendental thought has perpetual reference to transcendence and is therefore (in principle) open and inconclusive, the philosophising of idealism already implies the system— God himself is within it. In this way idealist thought is exposed as an illusion of movement within a self-contained repose. I find God present in my coming to myself; I become aware of myself, I find myself, i.e. I find God. The direction of intention is introspective. Whereas in genuine transcendentalism God's non-objectivity behind the activity of consciousness is such that the existentially God-intending act takes place in the *actus directus* but is inaccessible to the reflexion of consciousnesness on itself, in idealism the act is able to find God in the reflexion of conscious*ness* (*Bewusst-Sein*).[2]

The gospel of mind finding itself in God and God in itself

[1] Hirsch, *Philosophie des Idealismus*, p. 54.
[2] Brunstäd's distinction between the individual consciousness and universal conscious-ness (*Bewusstheit*), of which the former is a symbol, both coming together in the I, does nothing to alter the position. His attempt (op. cit., pp. 89–92) to reduce the interrelation of consciousness and *Bewusstheit* to that of the part and the whole, so as to ensure for *Bewusstheit* a being independent of individual consciousness (cf. p. 112f.), is arbitrary and leads straight back to realistic concepts.

was preached too seductively by idealism for theology to resist its blandishments, and all too readily it reasoned thus: if being is essentially consciousness, God must " be " in religious experiences, and the reborn I must find God in reflexion on itself. Where else could God be found but in my consciousness? Even if I can never pass beyond it, it must be what constitutes being in general. God, then, is the God of my consciousness. He " is " only in my religious consciousness.

But this was jumping to conclusions. If the philosophical system of idealism is the explicit form of pure mind coming to itself, an analogous theology would have to be the explicit form of reborn man's self-consciousness. But this latter, as a complex quantity, is essentially different from pure self-consciousness (which combines in the I the absolutely individual and the absolutely general); it is bound up with experiences of a particular content, and if God himself is to be found in this reborn consciousness he must be extracted from these experiences; yet this means that God once again becomes " objective " in the consciousness, consequently he is retracted into the unity of transcendental apperception, where he becomes the prisoner of the consciousness. Imperceptibly, God, who was to be regarded solely as a functional correlate of the mental act, has become the objective object.

There are two ways of recovery from this setback:

1. To radicalise the older thesis, from the standpoint of idealism, in such a way that the experience of God becomes the very self-experience of the transcendental I which is the basis of all other experiences. This course, to be sure, has only once been whole-heartedly adopted and developed on

39

a large scale—to the best of my knowledge. This was by
F. Brunstäd in his *Idee der Religion*. Here the point of
identity between God and man is presented in the idea of
the unconditional personality. The experience of God
must be the experience of this unconditional personality in
myself.[1] It follows that certainty of the experience of God
lies nowhere but in experience of the unity of my own I,
and, just as the transcendental unity of the I is the basis of
all truth, the truth of religion is confirmed only by the fact
that, in its character as experience of the unconditional
personality, it itself becomes the basis for the possibility of
all truth.[2] How the I can thereupon enter into communion
with God is something which cannot be explored, for plainly
here again God stands at any given time behind the I as
the basis of its possibility: if he could stand over against
the I he would have become an object. The I can never
say " God is " (as an object) without at the same time
saying " God is not ", i.e. not non-objectifiable, not permanently subjective. It is just the same with the I itself:
when I in fact say " I ", I could also say " God ". But just
as I can have no commerce with my transcendental I, I can
have none with God. The I keeps itself company; its

[1] Brunstäd, *op., cit.*, p. 151f.: " Religion as experience, as the being-
seized by awareness of the unconditional personality, of the unconditional value-reality of personal life, is the condition on which all
truth and validity is possible".

[2] Op. cit., p. 154: " The truth of religion does not lie in the fact that
science arrives at results coincident with the utterances of faith, but
in the significance of religious experiences, of *the* religious experience,
as a necessary prerequisite of all truth. Religious experience has a
certainty wholly in and through itself ". " Religion has truth, is truth,
because it comprises the basis of all possible truth in the experience of
the unconditional-synthetic unity of the I ".

looking into itself, into its inmost depths, is religion, but is also revelation of the divine mind, indeed that is all revelation is. What reason can learn from itself (thus Hegel) is revelation, and so God is incarcerated in consciousness.[1] Through living reflexion on itself, the I understands itself from itself. It directly relates itself to itself, hence to God, in reflexion. It follows that religion is here equivalent to revelation; there is no room for faith and Word, for they are repugnant to reason. Yet *Deus non potest apprehendi nisi per verbum* (A.C. 2, 67).

Here, as in the whole of idealism, the inmost identity of I and God, underlying everything, is simply an expression of the proposition: Like is conceivable only by like. If God is to come to man, man must already be in essence divine. If theology is to grasp the relationship of God and man, it can only do so by postulating the profound likeness of one to the other and finding there, exactly, the unity of God and man. One is like the very God one conceives.

Thus intensified, such propositions are exposed as theologically intolerable. It is not because man is by nature God that God comes to him—on the contrary, he would not then need to come—but because he is utterly unlike God and never shapes his concept of God according to his own image. That is why God gives himself to man, that man may conceive him, and then—only then—man can indeed

[1] Brunstäd would contest this (*op. cit.*, p. 214), but on p. 216 we read: " It (the unity of experience) *is* revelation, revelation in action; this very subjectivity, its very inwardness, is pervaded by and constitutes revelation "; and on p. 218: " We know God in so far as we are ' I ', in so far as we continue in experience. The limitation of our knowledge of God lies in the limited nature of our content of consciousness ". (!)

conceive him. This is an idea which has to find a place in Christian epistemology. Against it, however, the assumptions of the foregoing collapse. Everything clearly hinges on the transformation of ontological concepts into concepts of the act. In the first place, this operation leaves no other location to God but the I to be found in the execution of the mental act (or the basis of its possibility); secondly, the I is made the creator of the world. But, in the end, the philosopher has lost sight of the business of understanding the concrete psychophysical man—the man who is essentially at stake in Christian theology, and who invariably finds himself " already there " in his given world. The only thing which enabled idealism to achieve its resolution of ontological concepts was an unexpressed ontological judgment, and this produced a false position from the outset. The negative judgment of " this ' is ' not " or " this ' is ' only through me " remains in all circumstances an ontological judgment, and one, moreover, which does not lie within the confines of transcendentalism but represents a frontier violation with the most fateful consequences.

2. The second way of escape from the impasse is to fall back on the purely transcendental thesis. God is not objective. In this case that implies that he is no longer accessible even to the reflexion of consciousness on itself. He " is " in the pure execution of the mental act, but he stays withdrawn from every attempt to seize him in reflexion; he " is " as *actus directus*. The act is always " in reference to " transcendence, which means, in the transcendental framework, that " being ", independent of the I, is possible even if not given, whereas in idealism being and I merge one into the other. Unless the transcendental thesis is once

again to finish in the system of reason, it clearly requires a new version of the " bounds " of reason, viz. the concept of being and the concept of the act " in reference to " this being. For here is the reef on which the first attempt foundered.

Our own problem of being is not the problem of the existence or proof of a " real external world ".[1] No, we are concerned to ascertain the mode of being of divine revelation. In this context the meaning of the idea of transcendence, the meaning of the " outside " or of being, receives far clearer expression than in connection with the problem of the external world, however much both problems may coincide for idealism. The implications of the Christian idea of God, for example, for the question of the external world's reality, will receive attention in the positive section of this book.

The conceptual world of Karl Barth leans toward the

[1] If, to give an example, A. Riehl (*Der philosophische Kritizismus*, 2, pp. 1f. and 172) wishes to make the dependence of the consciousness on sensation the proof of the external world's reality, the logico-epistemological problems of idealism remain unaffected—even idealism does not doubt the existence of an empirical external world—but the argument lacks force as a contribution to epistemology, since it confuses psychological and epistemological significance. The same considerations disqualify the inference of the external world from " social emotions ". W. Dilthey's inquiry into the reality of the external world, which at first sight impresses as biassed in favour of tradition, proceeds from our experience of the will and resistance to it, and makes a thorough-going attempt to demolish the whole of idealistic epistemology in favour of a philosophy of life determined by history. Thus interpreted, Dilthey's work is of crucial importance for the most recent philosophy of history, and it has of late acquired influence over theology as well. (*Beiträge zur Lösung der Frage vom Ursprung unseres Glaubens an die Realität der Aussenwelt und seinem Recht*, 1890, Gesammelte Schriften, V, 1. Hälfte, pp. 90ff. and 134.)

transcendental theory.[1] But, in one way and another, the idealist encroachments on negative ontological judgments (*vide supra*), and their incompatibility with the idea of God, have nearly always been sensed, and frequently laid bare in full.

Likewise the epistemology of R. Seeberg [2]—in unmistakable contrast to that of Brunstäd—may be far more correctly denoted as Kantian-transcendental than as idealist; the same is true of his idea of religious transcendentalism. In the entire nexus of his ideas there are signs of the wrestling of theology with transcendental epistemology. Underlying all is an idea of God conceived as *actus purus*. In God there is no potentiality, only actuality; that leads Seeberg to pure voluntarism. God, the primal will, works as *actus* on man, and thus affects him, as a being whose nature is conscious mind, in his will. This encounter of God and man epistemology now tries to comprehend in transcendental terms. Though man is potentiality and act, while God is pure act, their encounter is evidently possible only in the act of awareness, therefore the essence of man lies in the mental act. It is however noteworthy that the term potentiality is plainly intended to provide for the concrete man, whom Seeberg believes himself unable to cover with the unmodified the idea of the act. Now, if God and man can meet only in awareness, i.e. in total freedom and full mental clarity as to the meaning of the process,[3] this is the point from which

---

[1] On this point cf. our chapter, " Revelation in terms of the act ".

[2] R. Seeberg, *Dogmatik*, I, especially pp. 70–110, 257–284.

[3] Op. cit., p. 103: " If the contact is to be a mental one, it cannot last for an instant without entering consciousness or becoming ideal "; p. 91: The contact of man and God happens in such a way that man

Seeberg can evolve his transcendentalism.[1]   As the consciousness " has " God, so he (God) " is "; if it " have "
him not, he " is " not.   What counts as valid is what is of
necessity thought by the subject.[2]   Being appears to be
submerging into act (somewhat in the manner of Brunstäd's
theory).   But at this very point Seeberg refrains from taking
the step to idealism.   On the contrary, we now find in his
argument bluntly juxtaposed statements which place the
existence of the supramundane—and of concepts to boot—
in the human mind alone, yet admit of no doubt as to an
" objective being ", i.e. a being of the supramundane which
manifestly transcends consciousness.[3]

This is the way in which the danger of identifying God
with the I is averted.[4]   God is the supramundane reality
transcending consciousness, the lord and creator.   This

" consciously and willingly himself performs, in consciousness of his
freedom, the movement performed in him by the mind of God ".

[1] Op. cit., p. 87: " But inasmuch as this mental entity is shown to
be real only in a particular disposition of man, and can be known by us
as real only in the form prescribed by this disposition, we shall have to
term the attendant sensation and knowledge ' transcendental ' ".

[2] Op. cit., p. 279: " The necessity of an item of subjective knowledge
is for transcendentalism the proof of the known thing's objective reality".

[3] Op. cit., p. 105: " And so, just as concepts *per se* are not in the
objective world but exist only in the mind of man, the supramundane
has no other existence than that it enjoys in the religious movements of
the human will, the religious intuition of the human mind.   In this
sense, here too, it is a matter of transcendental feeling and vision.   But,
just as transcendentalism does not cast doubt on the objective being
of the world, the ideas we here express do not cast doubt on the objective
being of the supramundane.   Only, this should be said: the super-
world is perceptible to the human mind—which is to say, existent—in
no other form than that of one specific mental apprehension".

[4] Op. cit., p. 93.

postulate is an unconditional requirement of Christian theology and is elaborated by Seeberg throughout his dogmatics. But on the other hand it can be said that God is existent only in the consciousness of man, or only *for* it. This is where Seeberg's theory of the religious a priori comes into play; man, he says, is " charged with the capacity " for " becoming directly conscious of pure mind ".[1] According to this theory, man is able to receive God into himself, i.e. to experience his immediate contact in feeling and intuition, and on these premises it is a thoroughly justified transcendental inference to attribute a being to God only in so far as a being-conceived corresponds to him. But at the same time it is also genuinely transcendental to refrain from an absolute negative judgment as to being; in the present case that restraint is exercised. Be that as it may, we are told of a direct becoming-aware, of God directly touching man. The religious a priori is said to be fundamentally open to the divine will, there is said to be a mould in man wherein the divine content of revelation may pour.[2] In other words, revelation must become religion, and that is its nature. Revelation is religion. But this represents a trend from pure transcendentalism to idealism, in that the absolute, to use Seeberg's terms, enters here again into " direct " contact, union, with the I, my will is subjected to the primal will and now God's will is

[1] Cf., op. cit., p. 81, Seeberg's self-dissociation from idealism.

[2] Op. cit., p. 104: " As a formal mental disposition, the religious a priori has no content of its own. The positive content of faith is dictated by revelation, the a priori is simply the intrinsic capacity, within this context, for becoming aware of the being and activity of the supramundane God, and accordingly for receiving the content of his revelation, as divine, into the soul ".

46

active in me. The difficulty lies in the idea of the religious a priori, in spite of the latitude Seeberg accords the concept. If we are to suppose that the urgent capacity to receive revelation is given with this a priori, i.e. in implication, the capacity of faith, that is already going too far. Natural man has a *cor curvum in se*. Even natural religion remains flesh, and strives after the flesh. If revelation is to come to man, he must be wholly transformed. Faith itself must be created in him. In this case there is no ability to " hear " before the " hearing ". These are thoughts which Seeberg himself expresses, and refers to in Luther.[1] But faith stands as the work of God, in a sense inapplicable to natural religiosity, for which the religious a priori noted by Seeberg certainly holds good. According to Luther, revelation and faith are bound to the concrete message, and the Word is the mediator of the contact between God and man, admitting no other " directness ". But then the idea of the a priori can only be understood to imply that certain mental forms are preposited for the formal understanding of the Word, in which case, it must be admitted, a specifically religious a priori loses meaning. All that pertains to personal appropriation of the fact of Christ is not a prioristic, but is owed to the contingent action of God on man. What Seeberg calls feeling (*Empfindung*) and intuition come under the same criticism, for the purely formal understanding of the Word requires no other noetic forms than are supplied by the a priori of thought itself.

In Seeberg's account of epistemology we find the clearest juxtaposition of theology's two great concerns: firstly, to affirm being transcendent of consciousness, and make

[1] *Dogmatik*, 2, pp. 506ff.

47

possible the formation of proper ontological concepts;
secondly, in the reference of revelation to the consciousness,
to expound the nature of the latter as act. It is a corollary
of these problems that not the transcendentalist-idealist
system, but only genuine transcendentalism, provides
philosophical concepts for their solution. However, it will
be later shown that even transcendentalism is inadequate
without radical transformation and completion.

2

THE ONTOLOGICAL ENDEAVOUR

Act pointed to being. Hegel restored the ontology that Kant had dethroned [1]; Kant's thing-in-itself was transformed into the concept of substance which Hegel found indispensable in defining mind.

It is the business of *true* ontology to prove the primacy of being over consciousness and to uncover this being. The immediate aim of ontology is no more than to say that there is " a real being outside consciousness, outside the sphere of logos and the limits of *ratio* "; " knowledge of objects refers to this being . . . but it is not coincident with this being ".[2] The proper problematic sphere of ontology is centred in its underlying concept. In the combination of logos and ὄν there is a clash of two equally mighty claims. The claim of logos, as presented in the preceding pages, is disputed by the ὄν which is in itself free. How, in these circumstances, is a science called ontology possible? Clearly it is only possible if one member of the combination—here it must be logos—desists from its claim, or in the case of

[1] Cf. *Enzyklopädie*, § 33.
[2] N. Hartmann, *Grundlagen einer Metaphysik der Erkenntnis*, 1925, pp. 180ff.

a *rapprochement* between the two. But this can only arise in the movement of thought, in such a way that the very movement of thought somehow partakes in essence of being. Here the step from Husserl and Scheler to Heidegger is foreshadowed.

If the logos does in fact surrender its claim, it abandons its system of immanence. The question is whether either, *per se*, is possible for logos. For, by an ironic subterfuge, logos may surrender only to recover with greater strength. Being, when it forms the content of intention (*Sein als gedachtes Sein*), remains an object "which *is* "—an entity. But the endeavour to regard thought itself as being is the test-case where transcendentalism, idealism and ontology must go their separate ways in decisions no longer imposed by intrinsic logic. The first imagines thought to " be " in " reference " to transcendence, idealism swallows up transcendental being into thought; finally ontology leaves being its full independence of thought, over which it also accords it priority. Genuine ontology, therefore, must always be a *critical* science, which does not even assume being as given—for being, which here includes even existence and quasi-hypostatic noesis (*Dasein und Denksein*), transcends the given, the entity—but thinks of itself as " already " existing only within the logos, in self-understanding; it is a science which forms ideas about this fact of " already existing " in context, and it is ever-mindful of the following correlation: at all times thought must be " suspended " in being.

Here the logos must voluntarily refrain from usurping creative power—whether it does so in true kenosis or in krypsis remains, of course, to be shown; spontaneity must, in consideration of being's independence, be transmuted into receptivity. In other words, insight or pure intuition (*intueri*=look upon, take note of) must evolve from creative thinking. And yet it is but a step from this position to *systematic* ontology, which throws being itself open to the inspection of intuition. This, however, is a flagrant retreat to behind the transcendental and idealist skepsis. Where thought or intuition have access to the object without need of mediation, there can be no genuine ontology, for this insists that thought is at all times " suspended " in being, therefore *critically* involved in the process of cognition.

Systematic ontology supposes pure being to be intuitively beheld in its transcendence of consciousness. Of course, if being should happen to be hiding behind phenomenal entities, thought will have the task of uncovering or " clearing the way to " this being. There are different ways of regarding this operation of laying bare " the essence ". But, in principle, man has eyes to see; he carries within him the possibility of penetration to the eternal essentials. In Platonic terms, he has beheld ideas, and now eternally bears *anamnesis* within him, until he attain pure vision once again. Man understands himself from what he has beheld, or sees the revelation of his own eternal nucleus. That is the unvarnished, unadulterated systematic ontology which has weathered modern philosophy unchanged, though expanded by Malebranche, in his doctrine of the participation of all knowledge in the idea of God, and later by the ontologism of Vincenzo Gioberti.

On the lines of the preceding chapter, the following pages

are intended to present a systematic ontology with the aid of a few salient examples.

In some way, the phenomenology of Husserl and his school, though it has an intense pre-occupation with ontological problems, is still within the pale of idealism. The consequences will be briefly shown. To Husserl [1] phenomenology is the study of the phenomena in the pure consciousness. It is only concerned with phenomena given to consciousness. From the outset, the question of existence is " put in inverted commas ". Realities and phantasmagoria vie together on the one level of consideration. Thereby arises a rift between essence and reality (*essentia*, that is, and *existentia*). To be sure, every act intends an object, consciousness is always " awareness of *x* ", but whether this " intentional object " envisaged by consciousness is also a real object is irrelevant to the question of pure essentiality. *Noesis* refers to *noema*, but the " noeto-noematic parallel structure " remains immanent in the consciousness. The empirical tree (for example) is not yet " given " in " simple perception " (*in* " *schlichter Anschauung* "), but before something can be " given ", the method of " putting in inverted commas " i.e. " phenomenological and eidetic reduction ", must be brought into operation. Thereby a way is found at once through theory to the pre-theoretic givenness. The simple givenness is marred by all interpretation, and anything real already represents interpretation, for reality is constituted by consciousness,[2] and so everything real must be absolutely

[1] *Logische Untersuchungen*, 1922 (Vols. 1 and 2 are particularly relevant). " Ideen zu einer reinen Phänomenologie", 1922.

[2] " Ideen zu einer reinen Phänomenologie," pp. 176ff., pp. 87–107.

" ruled out of bounds " [1]; thus phenomenological-eidetic reduction has the task of filtering away the empirical and factual from the *eidos*, the essence, so that the transcendental —no longer interpretative—consciousness and the essence stand over against each other in simple givenness. In both kinds of reduction, essential vision (*Wesensschau*), which is the specific cognitive method of phenomenology, comes into action. Just as there is a purely sensory, so there is a purely mental perception (*eine rein geistige Anschauung*). " The beholding of essences, it too, is perception, just as surely as the eidetic object is well and truly an object. . . . And so the beholding of essences really is perception—it is, moreover, beholding in the most meaningful sense, not a mere, more or less vague bringing to mind; thus it is a perception supplying the datum *at first hand*, seizing the essence in its ' corporeal ' selfhood." [2]

Here two trains of thought seem to cross paths in Husserl.[3] It is clear that the concept of essential vision implies that there stands over against the subject a being, independent of him and self-contained, whose concept he forms from direct vision, i.e. without interpretation or inventive production.[4] (What meaning could there be in reduction to the *eidos*, if in the end that too were understood to be a product of consciousness?) We may say that this train of thought

[1] idem, pp. 53ff.

[2] idem, p. 11.

[3] Attention has already been drawn to this, notably by R. Winkler's *Phänomenologie und Religion*, 1921 (pp. 63ff.), by J. Geyser's *Neue und alte Wege der Philosophie* and his *Max Schelers Phänomenologie der Religion*, 1924, and by W. Ehrlich in his *Kant und Husserl*, 1923.

[4] " Ideen zu einer reinen Phänomenologie," § 22 and § 24.

accords with a transcendental realism. Against this must
be set the contention that consciousness is the constituent
of all entities, i.e. the emphasis on the immanence in consciousness of all being. Only the regularity which consciousness projects *beyond* itself, so as to order reality within
it, is transcendent of consciousness.[1] But if this is the case,
the cognitive process can no longer be understood as
" vision " copying the *eidos* in " ideation "—even Husserl,
of course, rejects the realistic epistemology whereby consciousness is the mirror of being [2]—but must be represented
as creative, as " generating " this or that object (Cohen),
as spontaneity.[3] In other words, a priority belongs not on
the side of the object but on the side of the consciousness.
In this way Husserl joins hands with pure idealism in a
manner that seems to me quite at variance with his original
thesis. As for the idea of God, if one not unreasonably
expects from systematic phenomenology something re-
sembling the Platonic idea,[4] Husserl undeceives us by re-
quiring that God's transcendence should be put in inverted
commas.[5] Phenomenology poses no questions of *being*, only
questions of essence. Yet Husserl finds room in the question
of God for a passing reference, a kind of footnote, to the
possibility of some special " intuitive " intimation of God,
such as would require not a " mundane " concept of God
but a special form of transcendence.[6] Even if he here
attains no genuine clarity, the fact remains that Husserl's

[1] Idem, e.g. p. 96: Nature " is only as constituting itself on lines laid
down by consciousness ".
[2] Idem, pp. 185ff. [3] Idem, § 23, p. 42.
[4] Cf. *Logische Untersuchungen*, I, 2, § 64, p. 168.
[5] " Ideen zu einer reinen Phänomenologie", § 58.
[6] Idem, § 51, p. 96n.

phenomenology rests on belief in the possibility of intellectually mastering the absolute from out the pure consciousness—whether by means of the first-hand data of essential vision, or in some spontaneous manner. Nevertheless this is a belief which restores the I, the consciousness, to the place of God—which Husserl would deny, though it is an inescapable consequence of his philosophical premises. The ὄν has been overcome by the human logos, and there is no more arriving at truly grasped concepts of either being or God. Being as *existentia* is resolved in *essentia*, and the seal is set on the transition to idealism.

Now we see in Scheler how what Husserl confined to pure logic strives to embrace the " totality of life ". Evidently Scheler noticed the idealistic character of Husserl's phenomenology, and simply resumed the genuinely phenomenological thesis with the object, first, of purging it thoroughly of idealistic notions and, second, of developing it consistently in the fields of ethics and philosophy of religion. Where Husserl failed to prevent the emergence of a priority of logos over ὄν, despite his intention to preserve being's independence, Scheler reverses the position with his lucid elaboration of being's priority over consciousness. A decisive step was taken when he transferred the a priori from the formal and noetic to the supraformal, substantive, valuate and given,[1] which is a proper development from the basic premises of phenomenology. The object of inquiry is now no longer the general possibility of a priori data but the actual *quid-est* of the given.[2] Here—else there would

---

[1] *Der Formalismus in der Ethik und die materiale Wertethik,* 1921, pp. 43–87.
[2] Op. cit., p. 50.

be no philosophising—is an obvious postulation of being transcending consciousness. The question asked by Kantianism and idealism is dismissed as formalistic, therefore wrongly framed because laden with unwarranted assumptions. The datum present in values is there for the beholding in the rich fulness of every living thing, from the humblest to the highest values of the good and the holy.[1] But these values are predicates of being, i.e. such as inhere in a being, in logical independence of any consciousness; they lie displayed to the consciousness, just as conscious*ness* is displayed to the *conscious*ness. This moreover, as will be shown, has great significance for the doctrines of guilt, original sin and grace.

Turning to the idea of God, we find that God's transcendence of consciousness is preserved with the priority of being. God and I do not finally coalesce, yet two difficulties arise:

In the first place, it is a problem to discover how Scheler regards the actual existence of God, the positing of God's reality, and this is a question which remains unanswered not only in his *Formalismus in der Ethik und die materiale Wertethik* but also, upon inspection, in *Vom Ewigen im Menschen*. It appears as if Scheler takes as the object of his investigation the essence, but not the very existence, of God, and avoids proceeding to an affirmation of God's reality.[2]

---

[1] On this point cf. Przywara, *Drei Richtungen der Phänomenologie; Stimmen der Zeit*, 1928, and J. Geyser, *Max Schelers Phänomenologie der Religion*, 1924.

[2] See the opinions of J. Geyser, op. cit., pp. 35ff., and of E. Przywara in *Religionsbegründung*. Relevant pages are, in *Der Formalismus in der Ethik und die materiale Wertethik*, pp. 411. (especially n. 1), and, in *Vom Ewigen im Menschen*, pp. 541ff.

Scheler is unwilling to recognise as a proof of God's existence the fact that belief in the reality of God is given as part of the religious phenomenon. Such shyness in making statements about existence is of a piece with Husserl's way of putting reality in inverted commas. When Scheler opines that the demand for a proof of God outside the basic religious experience " is tantamount to asking that the existence of colours should be rationally demonstrated before they are seen, or of sounds before they are heard," [1] we indeed see clearly his will to posit reality, but we also see that the undertaking comes to grief in the same way as Cartesian methods of proof. Wherever he may stand in the matter, Scheler has difficulties with the problem of reality because, though he does not hesitate to base his thought on the hypothesis of the essence's transcendence of consciousness, he cannot find his way back to the *existentia* and finally loses his grip on the *essentia* as well.

The second difficulty stems from the question of how being and human logos—under which latter concept we may include the " sense of values "—are interrelated in the context of Scheler's theory. No doubt a sphere transcending the logos—not to say a primacy—is reserved for being, i.e. for the " essence ". Nevertheless, according to Scheler himself, in the " sense of values " the envisioning I is endowed with the capacity to take into itself the whole world, the fulness of life, the good and the very deity; by virtue of its vision of the highest values, it bears within itself, as a person, something which permits it to understand God and itself. In this way the being of God, of world and I is once again delivered into the hands of the person remaining

[1] *Vom Ewigen im Menschen,* pp. 551f.

57

in itself and understanding itself from itself. But this time
it is not as if the person produced the being, only as if the
being were accessible to the I from out itself,[1] as if man had
the power to confer and confirm the rightness, the justness
of himself and of the world.[2] Husserl leaves room for a
transcendence of God, without probing further. Scheler's
version of essential vision reaches out for God himself,
swings up to him in love, pulls him down to its own level—
this especially in the last period of Scheler's literary activity.
The All is sealed in by the I, and in this All there is also
God.

This well accords, even, with the " will to build a system " [3]
which at first seems incompatible with the bases of phenomenology, but is demonstrable in Husserl no less than in
Scheler. The goal of philosophy is not a " picture-book
phenomenology " but a system. A system, however, is
made possible only by an immanent idea of God, or by
total exclusion of the idea of God from the context of
philosophy—supposing that were a practical possibility,
which we would beg leave to deny. In the system there lies
the mastery of being by the knowing I, but hence also the
I's claim to divinity—" the path to the usurpation of godly
vision ".[4]

If previously God's mode of being was in question, it is
here determined, by the power of essential vision, to be

---

[1] *Der Formalismus in der Ethik und die materiale Wertethik*, p. 304, at the
foot.

[2] The original text has a play on the word *rechtfertigen*, to justify, which
is composed of *recht*, right or just, and *fertig*, achieved or complete—
Translator.

[3] *Logische Untersuchungen*, I, Chapter 11; *Formalismus . . . p. 7.*

[4] Przywara, *Drei Richtungen der Phänomenologie*, p. 262.

that of a phenomenal entity over against which the I stands in freedom of vision. Here the being which transcends the phenomenal entity, the very being whose mode thought intuitive vision know themselves to be, has been lost to sight, and the upshot is the system of pure immanence.

Phenomenology since Husserl has mishandled a problem whose clarification ought to have been indispensable for its very premises: the problem of being. Not until " reality ", the existence on which inverted commas have been so arbitrarily imposed, undergoes a new and radical onto-logical treatment, can we look for so much as a clarification of the act-being problem, on which Husserl and Scheler shed no light.

Here we have the point of departure for the most recent full-scale phenomenological investigation, which takes onto-logy itself as its object: Martin Heidegger's *Sein und Zeit*. In what appears to be the bluntest reversal of preceding phenomenology, *existentia* is made the *essentia* of *esse*.[1] Precisely where Husserl " puts in brackets ", Heidegger discloses being itself. Correspondingly, where Husserl and Scheler talk of timeless essentialities and values as the Being of the entity (in so far as this distinction is made!), in Heidegger Being is essentially interpreted in terms of temporality; and that again is only possible because the place of Husserl's " pure transcendental consciousness " is taken by the man himself concretely putting the question of being, the man who is withal an entity in the peculiar form of his own kind of Being: *Dasein*[2]. An understanding of being can only be gained by proceeding from a " hermen-

---

[1] *Sein und Zeit*, Halle, 1927, p. 42.
[2] *Dasein* means the entity which exists, namely, man himself.

eutics of *Dasein* ",[1] which is " analytic of the existentiality
of existence ". Being is understood from *Dasein*, since at all
times *Dasein* already " is in such a way that being is understood as something like Being ".[2] But, in all given instances,
Dasein is " my " *Dasein*. " Understanding of *Dasein* is itself
an ontological characteristic of *Dasein*". [3] *Dasein* is " being
in the manner of an understanding of being. That being
towards which *Dasein* can have such and such an attitude
or relation, and towards which it always does have some
kind of attitude or relation, we shall call existence". This
existence is not mere " Being-present-at-hand " (" *Vor-
handensein* ")—a mode of being not proper to *Dasein* but only
to the *res*—but is the already encountered decision and
realisation of *Dasein's* " potentiality for Being " (" *Sein-
können* "). " *Dasein* is not something ' present-at-hand '
which has also the endowment of potentiality in this or that
direction, but it is primarily potentiality. *Dasein* is what it
can be, and as it is its possibility to be." But great attention
must here be paid to the fact that Heidegger understands
the concept of possibility in a dual sense. His primary
concern is, as stated, the ontological analytic of the existentiality of existence, i.e. the " dissection of what constitutes
existence ".[4] So what are here brought to light are the
existential-ontological possibilities of existence; these must
be distinguished from the " ontico-*existentiell* " possibilities,
about which philosophy is silent. But neither kind of possi-

[1] Op. cit., p. 38.
[2] Idem, p. 17: " *in der Weise ist, seiend so etwas wie Sein zu verstehen*".
[3] Idem, p. 12: " *Seinsverständnis ist selbst eine Seinsbestimmtheit des
Daseins*".
[4] Idem, p. 12.

bility can be termed *absolute* possibility, for the very reason
that the existentiality of *historical* (*geschichtlich*) existence is
the object under review. " For its part, however, the
analytic of existence is in the last resort *existentiell*, i.e. rooted
in the ontic". [1] " The substance of man is . . . existence."
Dasein always finds itself already in a world. It is " being-
in-the-world " ; it is in " being with others ",[4] in " being
fallen into the ' they ' ", in everydayness. It understands
its " being-in-the-world " as its " having been thrown "
into the world. *Dasein* is the being-in-the-world of *Dasein*,
and its being, as potentiality, is epitomised in the proposition
that " existence is ' care ' " [5]—this too being understood in
a purely ontological-existential way. As temporal *Dasein*
within historicity (*Geschichtlichkeit*), it must order itself
upon its own final end, in order to attain its original wholeness. And this end is death.[6] In the most proper sense,
Dasein is " being towards death ". But instead of living in
this its proper condition of " commitment to death ",
Dasein always finds itself in process of " falling into the
' they ' ". But the call of conscience [7] summons *Dasein* to
rise " to its own very particular potentiality ". [8] And yet
the caller is *Dasein* itself, " finding itself thrown into the
world, and anxious about its potentialities ".[9] For *Dasein*
wishes to return to its true self, escaping the " uneasiness "
it feels in the world; in the call of conscience it understands
that it is guilty in its gravitation to the world, its futility,
and enters into the possibility most proper to it—commit-

[1] Idem, p. 13.   [2] Idem, p. 117.   [3] Idem, pp. 52ff.
[4] Idem, pp. 114ff.   [5] Idem, pp. 180ff.: " *Sorge*".   [6] Idem, pp. 235ff.
[7] Idem, pp. 270ff.   [8] Idem, p. 277.   [9] Idem, ibid.

ment to death. Yet this it does not by withdrawing from the world, but by taking its fallenness upon itself as its guilt. In this way *Dasein* lays hold of its most authentic possibility and its proper existence, inasmuch as it appropriates its own wholeness.

What is germane to our inquiry here is the unconditional priority accorded to the question of being over the question of thought: It has been the fundamental mistake of Descartes and all his followers to have neglected putting the question of being to the *sum* in " *cogito ergo sum* ".[1] But this question is not even possible unless there " *is* something such as understanding of being ".[2] All thought is but an ontological characteristic of *Dasein*. Thus even thought does not produce its world for itself, but finds itself, as *Dasein*, in a world; it is already in a world, just as it is already itself. Already *Dasein* is its possibility,[3] in authenticity or inauthenticity. It can choose itself in authenticity, or lose itself in inauthenticity. The decisive point, however, is that it already " is " whatever it understands itself to be and defines itself as. Here is obviously a leaning toward philosophical realism.[4] It is self-evident that *Dasein*, which is in the world, is in fact in a real external world. In this, realism is right, but it is wrong when it tries to prove this external world. " The scandal of philosophy does not lie in the fact that this proof has hitherto been wanting, but in the fact that such proofs are still awaited and attempted. ... Rightly understood, *Dasein* resists such proofs because

[1] Idem, pp. 22ff. and 211.

[2] Idem, p. 200.

[3] Idem, p. 42 (Grammatically, " its " may refer to " thought " or " existence "—*Translator.*)

[4] Idem, pp. 200ff., § 43.

in its being it already *is* what subsequent proofs consider still to require proving onto it". [1] An attempted proof presupposes an isolated subject on one side, and on the other an isolated entity. Being, however, can never be elucidated via entities, but can only be understood within *Dasein* (in the I-reflexion of idealism!).

So here, too, idealism gets its due. Being is essentially *Dasein*, but *Dasein* is mind [2] in its historicity. Nevertheless, passing beyond idealism, this *Dasein* itself must ask the question of its ontological structure, since only in this way can any light at all be shed on the meaning of being. [3] And so we have the priority of being over thought, yet being = *Dasein* = understanding of being = mind. That is how Heidegger's ontology finally takes shape for us. Being understands itself in *Dasein*, in mind. But *Dasein* is man's understanding in historicity, in the given temporal context of the decisions he has taken.

From the standpoint of the problem of act and being it appears that here the two members of the dichotomy are established in a genuinely consistent relation. True, the priority of being has finally assumed the character of a priority of mind-being, but not in such a way that mind annihilates being: it merely " is " and understands being. This solution, though reminiscent of Hegel, shows itself

[1] Idem, p. 205.

[2] Cf. Przywara on Heidegger, op. cit., p. 259: " The being of (human) mind is the absolute essence of being. . . . However much he may talk of reduction from truth to being Heidegger's being remains nothing other than the being of consciousness".

[3] Heidegger, op. cit., p. 208: " If the name idealism implies appreciation of the fact that being can never be explained in terms of entity, but is always ' the transcendental ' for every entity, then in idealism lies the one possibility of correct philosophical problem-formulation".

essentially distinct from his theory in that being is *Dasein*, " being in the world ", existing in temporality. Thus pure consciousness no longer dominates in Husserl's sense, nor in Scheler's the supraformal a priori. Heidegger has succeeded in forcing act and being into partnership in the concept of *Dasein*—that is to say, the actual decidings of *Dasein* coincide with its given decidedness. In non-decision, decision has already taken place. No absolute potentiality is attributable to *Dasein*. The ontological-existential structure cannot be wholly divorced from the ontic. And *Dasein* is not a discontinuous succession of discrete acts, yet neither is it the continuity of a supratemporal being. It is perpetual deciding in time, but also the constant *fait accompli*.

Two factors enable Heidegger to break through to this solution:

Firstly, he interprets being so thoroughly in temporal terms that even the eternity of God must, according to Heidegger, be thought of as, in principle, drawn into time, if it is to be philosophically considered at all.[1] Thus *Dasein* always " is " already, whenever it determines itself by decision. If on these occasions it were reaching down out of a sphere transcendent of time, it would always be having to constitute itself anew. " Being " is extricated from the static conception of the entity. It is explained with reference to understanding of being, thereby drawn into the flux of self-determining existence—what Dilthey calls the " totality of life ".

Secondly, temporal *Dasein* is always directed upon itself in self-decision, but this " itself " already " is ", so as to be able to decide itself. It is able to seize its most authentic

[1] See op. cit., p. 427, n. 1.

possibility, which it is offered by the existence it enjoys. It can arrive at itself, for it can understand itself; but this means that *Dasein* is included in the world, or rather that the world is included in *Dasein*.

It is the basic thesis of this ontological metaphysics that *Dasein* in temporality already possesses, at all times, understanding of being, that it is (so to speak) " open " to itself, and that *Dasein* in this way becomes insight into being. Thus the *genuinely* ontological development of the suspension of thought in being is permeated by the *systematic* theme of man's having, *qua Dasein*, an understanding of being at his disposal. Nevertheless it must be highly instructive for theology to see ready-formed in philosophy a metaphysical definition of the interrelation of act and being in which the concept of being remains self-contained despite its involvement in the internal reflexion of consciousness. Heidegger's philosophy is a consciously atheistic philosophy of finitude. It relates everything to the self-incapsulation, in *Dasein*, of the finite. It is cardinal for the existential analysis of *Dasein* that finitude should be conceived as sealed-in. *Incapsulation* can no longer be separated from finitude. Like all other existential characteristics of *Dasein*, its potentiality is revealed as determined by the incapsulation of the finite, not as a general existential constant of finite *Dasein* (*nicht als allgemeines Existential endlichen Daseins*). In its essence the philosophical concept of finitude is that of incapsulated finitude. Here, then, no room has been left for the idea of revelation, and with the knowledge in revelation that finiteness is creatureliness, i.e. is open to God, all concepts of being must be formed anew. It follows that Heidegger's concept of being, despite its powerful expansion of philosophy through discovery of the Existential sphere, cannot be adapted for the purposes of theology.[1]

Beginning with the anti-idealistic hypothesis of being's priority over consciousness, Catholic Thomism shatters the concept of basically closed being, in order to let in the transcendence of God. Within being, *esse* and *essentia* are rent apart.[2] While both coincide in God, so that one might wonder whether his existence comprehended his thusness, or his thusness his existence [3] (for God always *is* what he should be according to his essence), in man they are asunder. His *essentia* is related to his *esse*, but the latter always differs from it in some way, for man is in process of " becoming ", while God is " in being ". God is the eternal " Is " that is in all " Was " and " Will-be ",[4] yet is also infinite beyond them. It is not that the *esse* of man is divine and the *essentia* non-divine, nor the reverse, but the objective relationship of man and God lies in the former's *essentia-esse* difference and the latter's *essentia-esse* identity, considered together and as a whole. It takes the form neither of pure exclusivity (even if only partial) nor of pure identity (again, even if only partial), and the two sides of the relationship can rather be considered in a relation of " analogy ", as being is analogous to becoming. That is the Thomist principle of the *analogia entis*, which Przywara especially, in our time, has restored with methodical brilliance to the centre of Catholic philosophy of religion and dogmatics. By this thorough ontological treatment Przywara's Thomism appears

[1] Cf. also, op. cit., p. 61, n. 1.
[2] Cf. Aquinas: *De ente et essentia*.
[3] Przywara, *Religionsphilosophie katholischer Theologie*, 1927, p. 24.
[4] Przywara, *Ringen der Gegenwart*, Vol. 2, pp. 923ff.

to have succeeded in opening the concept of being to transcendence. God is not contained in existence, nor that in God, but just as God is imagined to exist absolutely in his own right, so man is envisaged as enjoying a relative but authentic reality of his own in relation to God (*causae secundae*): the concept of analogy demands two substances standing over against each other in relative independence of each other. But, as the " Is " stands " in-over " (" *in-über* "—Przywara's term) the becoming, and the latter " comes from " the former (" *von jenem her* " *ist*), God is not divorced from his creature, but is as much in him as he also allows him that relative reality of his own. (Thence arise the inferences of all-efficacy, as distinct from sole efficacy, the theory of the natural and supernatural, and the doctrine of grace.) This is the way in which Aquinas succeeds in interpreting existence in temporal terms without sealing it in itself. The question remains of whether the transcendence of God's " Is ", the analogy of divine being, is really adequate to express his transcendence as understood by Christianity, or whether, on the contrary, a metaphysics of immanence lurks behind the façade. The Thomist theory of being holds good for the being of man *qua* creature, inasmuch as his being is defined by St. Thomas as essentially creature-liness. This implies a continuity of the mode of being in both *statu corruptionis* and *statu gratiae*. With the continuity of his own ontological condition there is also guaranteed to man, by the *analogia entis*, a continuity of that of God, so that his being, whether in the original state of Adam or in Christ, can always be certain of its analogy to God's being. God is still " in-over " man; but if that is to acquire any kind of concrete theological sense and not remain purely formalistic and metaphysical, the modes of being " in Adam " or " in Christ " must be understood and interpreted in their own right; that is to say, we must ask whether there is in fact a being of man which is not already determined as his " being-in-Adam " or " being-in-Christ ", as his being-guilty or being-blessed-with-grace, and could not be understood only as such. But then, a priori, the ground is removed from under the possibility of a guarantee of divine continuity of being; the eternal Is remains a speculative idea which is continuously " in-over " becoming, which even admits of expansion into an a prioristic system of natural rational insight, but which is inadequate for a theological ontology. Primarily God is not the sheer Is: he " is " the just one, " is " the holy one, he " is " love. Theological concepts of being must have precisely this as their ontological premise, that the Is can in no way be detached from the concrete definition. Any formalistic attempt to fall back on " something of a more general nature ", supposedly discoverable behind the specific conditions of divinity, must serve to obliterate the Christian idea of revelation. The contingency of God's revelation in law and message is changed into a general theory of being with occasional modifications, and thus the path to a genuinely theological concept of sin or of grace is effaced. Only general attributes can be deduced from the concept of the analogy of being; the two like-unlike embodiments of being are fixed in their relational attitudes *vis-à-vis* each other; but from this standpoint, contingent action, whether of man or God, is unthinkable—everything, in principle, must already be preformed in the concept of analogous being. But now we come up against the Thomist concept of

existence, as epitomised in Przywara. Man, existing in the
esse-essentia tension, must bear within himself, as a given
existential possibility, the ability to behold the Is—the
esse-essentia identity. It follows from this, however, that in
this concept of existence one regards as implicit and already
" present " what remains only to be made explicit in those
ways of God to man (and vice versa) which are possible
within the limits of the *analogia entis*. But then human
existence is once more comprehensible through itself, and
it thereby also has access to God. That is the inevitable
consequence of all systematic metaphysics. Thus even the
attempt to open the concept of being to the transcendental
terminates in an illusory transcendence. There loom into
view the basic features of the ontological proof of God; if
there is a tension in the creature between *essentia* and *esse*,
there must be beyond that, underlying that tension and
making it possible, an identity of the pair: the divine being,
as *essentia* and *esse*. Just as Anselm arrived at a " being ", [1]
but, failing to arrive at God, remained in the closed
world, Thomist ontology is unable to advance beyond
an intramundane metaphysics in its concept of God, so
long as it purports to discover possibilities in man of understanding himself, and God via himself—in other words,
self-" projection on the lines of his authentic potentiality "
(Heidegger)—and so long as the world and its idea of God
are both contained within the I; but that means, so long
as there is failure to make room for a revelation, i.e. to form
theological concepts of act and being.

Does this indicate that every ontological thesis is useless for
theology? Such outright rejection is no more applicable

---

[1] Cf. Seeberg, *Dogmengeschichte*, III, 3, pp. 150f., n. 3.

here than in the case of the transcendental thesis. In so far as both—the act as foundation of being, and being as foundation of act—evolve into the I-enclosed system (in that the I understands itself from itself, can place itself in truth), they offer no assistance in understanding the idea of revelation. If on one side the genuinely transcendental thesis admitted a being transcendent of consciousness, a being " with reference " to which existence was envisaged, but a being which itself remained non-objective, and if on the other side genuine ontology considers being the a priori of thought in such a way that thought is itself suspended in being, it is an inescapable conclusion that in the first case the limits are prescribed by reason itself, that in the second case being somehow falls into the power of the thinking I, consequently that in both cases the I understands itself from itself within a closed system. *Per se*, a philosophy cannot spare room for revelation [1]; let it then recognise revelation and confess itself Christian philosophy, knowing that the place it wished to usurp *is already* occupied by another—Christ.

Nevertheless, it may be that in the following pages we shall find in genuine transcendentalism and ontology (as distinct from idealism and phenomenology) certain contributions to the solution of the act-being problem *within* the concept of revelation, if only because they have exhaustively fathomed and argued the philosophical dilemma of act and being, or because we shall be able to adopt their polar standpoints of man as pure act " with reference to ", and thought " suspended " in being, in order to test against revelation, in the sharpest possible antithesis, the merits of

[1] See Note concluding Part One, pp. 73ff.

70

explanation in terms of act or of being. If that is so, we may be sure that these theories will emerge from their encounter with the idea of revelation in a wholly new guise, but equally we shall know that the " with reference to " and the " suspension " are amenable to theological inter-pretation, hence, after all, of service in understanding the idea of revelation.

What offends Christian thought in any autonomous self-understanding is that it considers man capable of bestowing truth on himself, of transporting himself into the truth by his own resources, since it is reasonable to suppose that the " basis " of existence must somehow be within truth (likeness to God). Here, however, " truth " comprises only that reference to God which Christian theology does not hold possible save in the *Word* spoken, of man and to man, in the law and the gospel. It is in this sense that formal validity may be conceded to the proposition, common to transcendentalism and idealism, that knowledge about oneself or about God is no " disconnected possession ",[1] but places the knower in a direct " possessive " relation to the known; employing a terminology which must be further explained below, this means that knowledge in truth about oneself, or about God, is already " being in . . ."—whether in " Adam " or in " Christ ".

" Never being able to give oneself truth " represents the unattainability of a systematic metaphysics; for such knowl-edge as that would imply would signify a self-placing into the truth. But neither is such knowledge a possibility for

[1] Cf. F. K. Schumann, *Gottesgedanke und Zerfall der Moderne,* 1929, closing chapter.

71

any " critical philosophy " [1]; a philosophy with such great expectations of itself would be highly uncritical. Thought is as little able as good works to deliver the *cor curvum in se* from itself. Is it merely by chance that the profoundest German philosophy finishes in the I-confinement of the All? No, the knowledge it represents is likewise a self-placing into truth—for the world of the I untouched by grace is confined to the I—though not the truth of God's word, because it simply " is " not in this truth; if it were, it would be unable to celebrate here the triumph of the I, but would have to recognise, in its eternal loneliness, the curse of lost communion with God. Only thought which, bound to the obedience of Christ, " is " *from* the truth—can place into the truth. Thus our way is pointed onward to revelation itself, yet we cannot understand this step merely as a final possible step, but as one which must already have been taken, or us to be able to take it.

This is something which very recently a group of theologians and philosophers, whose ideas join in circling round the central problem of existence, have understood and accepted. It remains to be seen, of course, whether they have succeeded in adequately interpreting the idea of revelation from the standpoint of the act-being problem.

[1] Cf. the passage on Grisebach in Part Two.

NOTE

Theological anthropology

If P. Tillich is of the opinion that no distinction can be made between philosophical and theological anthropology (*Religiöse Verwirklichung*, Furche, n.d., p. 300), one need only indicate in reply the concept of revelation. If from the standpoint of revelation the existence of man is seen by a theological anthropology as essentially determined by guilt or by grace—and not merely as "being at risk (*Bedrohtheit*) in the unconditional sense"—philosophical anthropology is able to avail itself of those concepts only at the cost of bursting its frame, of transforming even this analysis of human existence into an attempt to seize hold of itself, of—in other words—becoming theological anthropology. Admittedly, this does nothing to settle the question of truth. This may be put to the test only in conjunction with the concept of contingency inherent in revelation. Cf. relevant passages below, also F. Gogarten, " Das Problem einer theologischen Anthropologie " in *Zwischen den Zeiten*, No. 6, 1929. Recently R. Bultmann (" Die Geschichtlichkeit des Daseins und Der Glaube," *Zeitschrift für Theologie und Kirche*, 1930, No. 5, pp. 339–64) has formulated the interrelation of philosophy and theology in such a way that it becomes the business of philosophy to investigate phenomenologically those structures of existence (*Dasein*) which represent the existential-ontological (as distinct, of course, from ontic) possibilities of believing and unbelieving

73

existence alike. " Philosophy sees that existence is in all cases a concrete existence characterised by a definite 'How'; it speaks of the ' actual fact ' of this ' How ', but not of the ' How itself' " (op. cit., p. 342). The theme of philosophy is said to be existentiality, that of theology concrete (believing) existence. The same line is followed by the following statements on the concept of revelation: No believer can say more exactly or completely than an unbeliever what revelation is. " What ' more ' does the believer know? Just this, that revelation has descended upon him, that he is in life, endued with grace and forgiven " (op. cit., p. 352). The event-character of revelation and the event-character of belief can, notwithstanding their contingency, be imagined within the existential-ontological possibilities of existence. The precondition for all this is to be found in Bultmann's unpursued assertion that " existence in faith is still, in any case, existence " (op. cit., p. 343). But this is the very point where further questions ought to be asked, for here lies the root of philosophy's infinite claims. The question is whether one can assert this uniformity of existence irrespective of revelation (be it only the uniformity of existential-ontological possibilities) without making revelation superfluous. If one can, then the believer does in fact know nothing " more " about revelation, in principle, than the unbeliever. But the position is otherwise when seen from the standpoint of revelation itself: the believer knows everything about revelation whereas the unbeliever knows nothing; the reason is that the essence of revelation lies in its character as a contingent event. For the purposes of existential-ontological analysis, revelation may be envisaged among the standing possibilities of existence, but then it does not possess its essential character of an event—one originating in God's freedom. Only where forgiveness of sins is an event do I know of revelation as a believer, and where that event does not take place, the forgiveness of sins of which I " know " is not *the* forgiveness of sins attended by revelation: if this were not so, the doctrine of justification would be tottering. But if revelation is essentially an event brought about by the free act of God, it outbids and supersedes the existential-ontological possibilities of existence. *Then* there is no longer an essential identity of existence *per se* in all instances—whether the event of revelation has taken place or not. *Then* revelation claims to initiate the unity of existence and to have sole right to proclaim it; philosophy sees the deepest root of its claims excised. The abandonment of the ontic by retreat upon the ontological is considered inadmissible by revelation. In the existential event of revelation the existential structure of existence is attacked and transmuted. There is here no second mediator, not even the existential structure of existence. For revelation, the ontic-existential and the ontological-existential structures coincide. Inasmuch as it consistently observes man without regard to the event of revelation, the phenomenological definition of existence according to its existential structure as " historical ", as " care ", as " being unto death ", is, for revelation, no less an abstraction and hypothesis than a merely biological definition of man. That is why, finally, this interpretation of existence is also irrelevant to theology. (Cf. especially Kurt Löwith, " Phänomenologische Ontologie und protestantische Theologie " in the *Zeitschrift für Theologie und Kirche*, 1930, No. 5, pp. 365–99. I find myself very largely agreeing with him against Bultmann

75

in what he has to say about the preformed " ideal of
existence " underlying even existential analysis, in point of
which the general idea of existential analysis is widely
open to criticism: I have greatly profited from Löwith's
article.)

PART TWO

<hr>

The act-being problem in Revelation, and the Church as its solution

REVELATION IN TERMS OF THE ACT

A. *The contingency of revelation*

The proposition that man cannot place himself into truth is not self-evident in the sense of entitling or obliging one to postulate *thenceforth* a revelation capable of supplying truth. On the contrary, the untruth of human self-understanding is obvious only from the viewpoint of revelation and *its* truth, once it has taken place and been accepted in belief. Were it not so, revelation, as the final postulate of human thought, would itself be ensnared in the falsehood of self-understanding, with the result that man, from the postulates of his own existence, would enter the position of adjudging himself right and placing himself into truth— which nevertheless the revelation he postulates, if fully intended as real, is alone able to do for him. Consequently, only the person already placed in truth can understand himself as in truth. For from within truth he can, in his potential reproduction of his " being known " by God (cf. p. 32 above), understand or recognise that he is situated in truth, i.e. re-created from untruth into truth. But only from within truth, i.e. in revelation, which is to say, whether judged or pardoned, in Christ. This is what yields the theological concept of existence: existence is envisaged in reference to revelation, as encountered or not encountered by revelation. There is no longer any inherent potentiality of being encountered: existence either is or is not actually encountered by revelation, and this happens to it, as a concrete, psychophysical whole, on the " borderline " which no longer passes through man as such, or can be drawn by him, but is Christ himself. This concept of existence will have to be made explicit in the following pages, and attest its own validity in various connections.

It is in this frame of reference that one should envisage the agenda of all theology, which ever since Duns Scotus and William of Occam has laid special stress on the contingency of revelation; but in the contingency of revelation is asserted its transcendence of reason, i.e. its absolute freedom in relation to reason, likewise to all possibilities deployable, so to speak, by an existence understood as potentiality. Revelation, which places the I into truth, i.e. gives understanding of God and self, is a contingent occurrence which can only be welcomed or rejected in its positivity—that is to say, received as a reality—but not elicited from speculations about human existence as such. It is an occurrence with its basis in the freedom of God, whether positively, as his self-giving, or negatively, as his withholding of himself.

The proposition of God's freedom in revelation admits a double interpretation. First, a formal one: God is free inasmuch as bound by nothing, not even by the manipulable " entity " of his " historical " Word. The Word as truly God's is free. God can give and withdraw himself absolutely according to his pleasure; in either action he remains free.

He is never at man's discretion; it is his honour and glory [1]
to remain utterly free and unconditional in relation to
everything given and conditional. " Now it would follow
that the relationship between God and man in which God's
revelation may truly be imparted to me, a man, must be
a free, not a static relationship, in the sense that its very
constancy may never mean anything other than constancy
in a transaction not only continuous but at every moment
beginning, in all seriousness, at the beginning. It may
never be conceived as already given, already obtaining, nor
even as analogous to a natural law or mathematical function;
instead, one must always think of it as *actwise (aktuell)*—
i.e. with all the instability of a deed in course of execution ".[2]
Revelation is interpreted purely in terms of the act. It is
something happening to receptive man, but within God's
freedom to suspend the connection at any moment. How
could it be otherwise, since it is " God's pleasure, majestically
free " (Barth) which initiates the connection and remains
its master. God is understood as pure act. God's freedom
is the possibility—but with all that *possibility* implies—
comprehended in the concrete act.

Inevitably, exception must be taken from the first to the
fact that the God-man relationship should be resolved in
terms of pure act-subjects in the very context where revelation's transcendence of consciousness is unequivocally
asserted. And the suspicion therefrom arising, that trans-

[1] But cf. Luther, W. A., 23, 157: " It is the honour and glory of our
God (*unseres Gottes Ehre*), however, that, giving himself for our sake in
deepest condescension, he passes into the flesh, the bread, our hearts,
mouths, entrails, and suffers also for our sake that he be dishonourably
(*unehrlich*) handled, on the altar as on the Cross ".

[2] Barth, *Dogmatik*, I, 1927, p. 295.

cendentalism is lurking here somewhere, receives confirmation. God reveals himself only in acts freely initiated by himself. " Man is touched with grace when, and from the fact that, the Word of God comes to him, no sooner, no later, and not otherwise. So far as is known, the heavenly manna in the wilderness could not be put into storage ".[1] God's Word has no being in independence of his self-revelation to man and its being heard and believed by man. This, however, is where we may recognise the transcendental thesis. Because God himself creates the hearing and belief, and is indeed himself hearing and believing, in man,[2] "God's Word is only in the act of belief, never in that abstraction from the strictly occasional event, at God's sole discretion, which we call grace." [3] God's being is solely act,[4] is consequently in man only as act, and that in such a way that any reflexion on the accomplished act has *ipso facto* lost contact with the act itself, with the result that the act can never be grasped in conceptual form and cannot therefore be enlisted into systematic thought. It follows that although Barth has no hesitation in making use of temporal categories (moment, here and now, before, after, etc.) his concept of the act must not be regarded as temporal. The freedom of God and the act of belief are essentially supratemporal; if Barth nevertheless stresses the act which, recurrently " beginning at the beginning ", is at all times free, so that there can be no inference from one act to the next, we must

[1] Barth, " Schicksal und Idee in der Theologie", in *Zwischen den Zeiten*, 1929, No. 4, pp. 324f.

[2] Barth, *Dogmatik*, I, pp. 357f. Also *Zwischen den Zeiten*, 1925, No. 3, pp. 239ff.; *Dogmatik*, I, pp. 284ff.

[3] Barth, in *Zwischen den Zeiten*, 1929, p. 325.

[4] Idem, p. 321.

understand that he is endeavouring to translate the transcendental concept of the act into terms of the *geschichtlich*.
However, this attempt is bound to come to grief against the
fact that (according to Barth) no " historical " moment is
capax infiniti, so that the empirical action of man—" belief ",
" obedience "—becomes at most a pointer to God's activity
and can never, *in* its historicality, be faith and obedience
themselves.

Thus the problem of transcendental philosophy, which
we discovered at the beginning, presents itself afresh. God
recedes into the non-objective, the non-available. That is
a necessary consequence of the formal conception of his
freedom, which might be traced without difficulty to the
combination of nominalism and the idea of contingency in
the closing stages of medievalism.[1]

God remains always the master, always the subject, so
that if any man should think he has God as an object, it is
no longer *God* whom he " has "; God is always the " coming ", not the " existing " deity (Barth).

It was inevitable that this formal understanding of God's
contingent activity should lead Barth to develop his idea of
the " dialectical ". " God's Word is not bound, and never
will be bound. Theological dialectic is genuine dialectic
to the extent that it is open to this idea, to the extent—in
fact—that it will subserve this idea, subserve the freedom of
the Word of God ".[2] The freedom of God's Word cannot

[1] Admittedly, the late-scholastic concept of God's freedom appears to
refer only to unreal possibilities. In that way the positivity of ecclesiastical order could be preserved. According to Barth, however, the
freedom of God persists within the positive order, with a rider of explosive
possibilities for all historical forms.

[2] Barth, in *Zwischen den Zeiten*, 1929, p. 346.

be pinned down by unequivocal theological statements. It
snaps their pronouncement in twain: thus there are only
theological statements under " critical reservation ".[1] All
Barth's theological propositions are rooted in the necessity
of saying *not-God* when I speak of God (because *I* speak of
him), and *not-I* when I speak of the believing I; thus due
regard is paid to the idea that genuinely theological concepts
do not fit into an undialectical system—if it were otherwise,
concepts of an act-character would have petrified, within the
system, into fixed ontological abstractions, and the concept
of contingency would be excluded: the " coming " changed
to the " existing " God. Revelation would have sunk to
rest in the theological system. This is countered by the
critical reservation. But it is not as if the " systematic "
formula for a theology of revelation had at last been found
in a dialectical theology; no, " for theology too, there is a
justification only by faith ".[2] The reservation made by
dialectical theology is not a logical one, such as might be
suspended in the antithesis, but one real and recurrent in
view of predestination[3]; however, as such no theological

---

[1] R. Bultmann derives his concept of dialectic from the historicality
of existence, and I feel this entitles one to say, while acknowledging the
difference between their concepts of existence, that on this point there
is no fundamental difference between him and Barth. Man in the
historical situation proposes, or " is ", the question to which God gives
his free answer, and the only way to talk about this answer in historicality is " dialectically ". " Dialectical " does not mean so much
" determined by the object " as " determined by the historical reality "
—by the concrete question of the situation, and by God's answer. See
Theologische Blätter, 7th Year, No. 3, p. 66.

[2] Barth, in *Zwischen den Zeiten*, 1929, p. 348.

[3] The reproach cast up against Barth by Grisebach and his friends,
that at bottom he has a catholicising influence, because even his theology

idea can ever seize God: it remains, " strictly speaking, a
testimony from the Devil ".[1] God remains free, non-
objective, pure act, but he can, if he choose to do so, make
use of a theology in order to attest himself therein. That
does not lie within the power of the theology but, again,
within the freedom of God. Thought is a cohesive whole,
incapable of radical self-disturbance; of this Barth is
conscious—that even dialectical theology is no way to catch

---

of the reservation is a system—with the mere difference of including
a reservation—seems to me, quite apart from an untenable philosophical
and theological assumption which is mentioned in the text, to do Barth
an injustice. One cannot determine to achieve the theology of the
Word, " one can only *be* determined in the direction of the theology of
the Word. . . . Not because my dialectic might be supposed so superior
in quality, but because God wishes to make use of me and that question-
able instrument, thus not because I have found the philosopher's stone,
squared the circle, traced the line of intersection of the two planes,
reality and truth, . . . but because it has pleased God to make himself
known to me " (Barth, in *Zwischen den Zeiten*, 1929, p. 347). If H. M.
Müller (" *Credo ut intelligam;* Kritische Bemerkungen zu Karl Barths
Dogmatik", *Theologische Blätter*, 1928, No. 7) and Gerhard Kuhlmann
(" Zum theologischen Problem der Existenz", *Zeitschrift für Theologie
und Kirche*, 1929, No. 1, p. 33, n. 1) think that Barth's critical reservation
constitutes his systematic method, I myself feel compelled to take a
different line of interpretation. Theological cognition can " never
catch God " (Barth, op. cit.). It is only possible that God should make
himself known to it of his own free will. Both sides of the proposition
are meant in an existential (*existentiell*) sense; thus the negation does
not purport to embody the secret way to the universal truth about God,
the way to the system, but the witness of obedient thought, which
must be testified anew on every occasion. As will be seen, there is a
further inference, which will be discussed subsequently in the text, to
the effect that there must be obedient theological thinking, even without
the critical reservation.

[1] Barth, in *Zwischen den Zeiten*, 1929, p. 348.

God. How could it be otherwise, since before all thought stands unfathomable predestination?

This attempt at unsystematic thinking, corresponding to God's freedom as formally understood, finds its parallel in a new trend of philosophy, which itself takes part with lively interest in the development of modern theology. E. Grisebach [1] has tried in various works to clarify the idea of —or rather, point the way to—reality: every system, in one way or another, conflates reality, truth and the I; purports to understand reality and have it at its disposal. In his " satanity ", man is tempted to draw reality, the absolute, his fellowman, into himself, but in this way he remains alone with himself in his system, and fails to arrive at reality. Theory is unable to form a concept of reality. Reality is " experienced " in the contingent fact of the claim of " others ". Only what comes from " outside " can show man the way to his reality, his existence. In " sustaining " the " claim of my neighbour " I exist in reality, I act ethically; that is the sense of an ethics not of timeless truths but of the " present ".[2] Man can never have the absolute at his disposal, i.e. bear it within him, and for that reason he never arrives at the system.

Friedrich Gogarten and H. Knittermeyer have developed this thesis for theology in such a way that the place of man's encounter with the absolute, with God, is taken by his encounter with the Thou of his neighbour, his restriction

[1] Cf. especially *Die Grenzen des Erziehers und seine Verantwortung*, 1925, and *Gegenwart: eine kritische Ethik*, 1928.

[2] On Grisebach's concept of time, cf. *Gegenwart*, Chapter 12, " Vom Gestern, Heute und Morgen ".

by the other as working itself out in history—if not actually constituting history.[1] Faced with this Thou, all " humanistic-systematic " thought, tending to ontological concepts, must confess its impotence. For we are dealing with history: that is, the meeting of I and Thou. The meaning of the gospel is that the claim of one's neighbour was met once and for all in Christ.[2]

Undeniably, the objection to be raised against this thesis is that in the attempt to avoid any postulation of an absolute, the Thou is in effect made absolute. If the I's claim to be absolute is to be transferred merely to the Thou, not to him who is above both and above the absolute, we appear to be heading for a wholly ethicalised version of the gospel; worse, even the concepts of history and theology are growing obscure, which means that revelation is being lost to sight.

[1] Tillich's theories also concentrate on the frustration of man. But he does not advance beyond the speculative in his attempt to define the nature of the Protestant message, firstly, as the drive " to live-through the impasse of one's limitations (*die Grenzsituation*) " and, secondly, as " the pronouncement of the Yes, which befalls man when he takes his *Grenzsituation* with utter seriousness " (*Religiöse Verwirklichung*, p. 40; his third definition is irrelevant here); the same may be said of his rejection of all " religious contents, even God and Christ " (p. 38). Speaking in concrete terms, what else is man's *Grenzsituation* but sin; and what else is the Protestant message to preach but the " religious content " of grace and forgiveness of sin? But the *Grenzsituation* must be preached to man with the Word of judgment and mercy. If I could transplant myself into truth without the aid of the message, I could place myself in truth of my own accord, and *lumen naturae* would be justified in itself.

[2] The " Dogmatics " of both Gogarten and Knittermeyer begin from this viewpoint (respectively, *Ich glaube an den dreieinigen Gott*, 1926, and *Die Philosophie und das Christentum*, 1927). Cf. Gogarten in *Zwischen den Zeiten*, 1929, No. 6.

Now if, as stated, the I is called into reality by the Thou, if the Thou shows it the way to its existence, this certainly appears to open to Thou and I a possibility of being and understanding themselves in reality, of reciprocally " placing " each other " into truth ", without God and revelation. If this is so, the possibility is based on postulation of the Thou as absolute, and it therefore follows that such a " critical " philosophy is useless as a theological hypothesis, for the one hypothesis of theology is that revelation is man's only possibility of entering truth.[1] Thus Grisebach's critical philosophy, because " ideal " even while critical, remains a system. Even if it could be genuinely " unsystematic ", it would still appear to trap reality, to enter reality from its own resources. Thought, if it is genuine thought, is bent on completeness, for thought is even able to comprehend the claim of " the other ". Grisebach is right, and comes a long way to meet Christian thought, when he says that man can be shown the way to reality only from outside. But the natural man's first intimation of this " from outside " is not supplied by his contact with his neighbour's claim, even though it is his reaction to this which finally enables him to exercise moral conduct; no, it is supplied by his encounter with something that at the same time enables him to understand the " from outside " in a meaningful sense—revelation accepted in faith.

The will to refrain from a system, as a deliberate gesture of ethical modesty towards others, is no more a prerequisite

[1] Man can be " in reality " and " in truth " only through God. True reality is reality seen through the truth of the Word of God, so that whoever is in reality is also in truth, and vice versa.

than good works for the understanding of revelation. God-
less thought—however ethical—remains self-enclosed. Even
a critical philosophy is powerless to place the philosopher in
truth, because its criticism issues from itself, and the seeming
reality is still subservient to the (in this case undemanding)
claims of the *cor curvum in se*. Revelation is its own donor,
without preconditions, and alone has the power to place in
reality. From God to reality, not from reality to God, goes
the path of theology. Accordingly the will to refrain from
a system must fail in its purpose; thought stays within itself,
in sin as in grace. That thought is bent on a system, cannot
disrupt itself, is self-contained, that is its property by reason
of its creation and its eschatological end, where it no longer
needs self-disruption because it is in reality, placed by God
in truth eternally, because it sees. But for that reason any
system of man which *is* not eternally in truth is an untrue
system and must be broken in pieces that the true system
may become possible. It is the preaching of the Word that
brings about this breakage through faith. And so we come
to the problem of theology, predication and faith, which is
treated at greater length below.

In sum: all thought remains in itself so long as existence
remains in itself. But revelation, the Word, leads existence
out of itself into a state of self-criticism. Even when existence
has been placed in truth, its thinking about itself and God
remains within itself, but is repeatedly disturbed by the
reality of revelation in a way which distinguishes it from
profane thought, as will later be explained; this means that
man must have *been* placed in reality by God if there is to
be a place for reality in his thought.

If the knowledge of God and self divinely implanted in

man is considered purely as act, any being is of course
wholly excluded. The act is always inaccessible to reflexion;
it fulfils itself always in " direct consciousness " (see above).
That follows from the formal understanding of God's
freedom. In this way theological thought seems condemned
to remain in principle profane; it can only, in the event,
stand " under the sign of God " (thus Barth). But the
following objection has to be made: what can it mean to
say that theology requires a justification by faith (see p. 84
above), when it can only be a question of justifying the
theologian who thinks the theology? Indeed it is open to
doubt whether the existence of the theologian, placed in
truth, serves to distinguish his systematic thought from
profane thought, whether there is any such possibility at all
(if so, on what basis?) Seen from the viewpoint of a formalistic understanding of God's freedom, the theory of revelation as pure act can only serve to deny the possibility of a
distinction between profane and theological or—if we may
anticipate—ecclesiastical thought.

The whole situation impels one to ask whether a formalistic
understanding of God's freedom in contingent revelation,
conceived wholly in terms of the act, is really the proper
groundwork for theology. In revelation it is a question less
of God's freedom on the far side from us, i.e. his eternal
isolation and aseity, than of his forth-proceeding, his *given*
Word, his bond in which he has bound himself, of his freedom
as it is most strongly attested in his having freely bound
himself to historical man, having placed himself at man's
disposal. God is not free *of* man but *for* man. Christ is the
Word of his freedom. God *is there*, which is to say: not in
eternal non-objectivity but (looking ahead for the moment)

" haveable ", graspable in his Word within the Church. Here a substantial comes to supplant the formal under- standing of God's freedom. If it should prove itself, it will suggest a redirection of our attention from revelation seen in terms of the act towards ontological ideas. But we may be sure that from the new standpoint, with its reappraisal of revelation, the problem of the theological system will assume quite a different aspect and resolve itself in quite a different way. It would remain to be seen to what extent one would still be justified in using concepts of the act to explain revelation.

But first of all we shall examine the epistemological problems deriving from act-theory in this context, and subse- quently observe the concept of existence from the same viewpoint, after which the state of the case will demand that we proceed to ontological theory.

B. *Knowledge of revelation*

The explanation of revelation in terms of the act has its philosophical counterpart in the genuine transcendental thesis. Epistemologically this signifies that one can speak of the object of knowledge only with reference to the cogni- tive subject. Essentially nothing is thereby said about the being of the entity outside its being known. The transcen- dental can never become the object of knowledge; being the basis for the possibility of all cognition, it evades the cognitive act because it is, precisely, the pure act in cogni- tion. Anything objective is involved in or formed by cognition; all that remains free of the I is the basis of the known as of the knower; in other words, being, unlike the entity, is not involved in the I but transcends it. The identification of being and the I, precipitately inferred by idealism, is impossible once the I recognises that it exists in time, bound to its existence in history.

If we now try to place revelation in this frame, we have the one choice of considering it objective or non-objective. Epistemologically, it certainly appears that we must place it in the non-objective, for the objective is involved in the I, in which case the being of the entity, as we have seen, retains its freedom but cannot become objective. Yet if revelation is non-objective, the theological implication is that God always remains a subject and evades every human attempt to seize him cognitively. If, on the other hand, we are really speaking of *revelation*, it must somehow, by definition, become manifest to man, knowable by man; and in fact God's revelation has, as we know, become knowable in Christ. How are we to understand that? God can never become the object of consciousness. Revelation can only be understood in such a way that God must be borne in mind as a subject; but this is possible only if God is also the subject of the knowing of revelation, since, if *man* knew, then it was not God that he knew. But this knowing of revelation is called " believing ", what is revealed has the name of Christ, the subject of the understanding is God as the Holy Spirit. So in revelation God is in the act of understanding himself. That is his location, and he cannot be found in my consciousness for any reflexion on this act. Essentially, the representation of God which I have in my consciousness is not God himself. God is only in the act of belief. In " my " belief, the Holy Spirit is accrediting himself. That this is so is no demonstrable matter of fact but is merely "existentially" true, i.e. in the encounter with revelation, in the act of belief itself, which for the rest remains an act psychic like the others. Accordingly my knowledge of God depends in the event on whether God has known me in Christ (I Cor. 13, 12; Gal. 4, 9), whether he is effecting faith in Christ within me. There is therefore no prescriptive method for acquiring knowledge of God; man cannot transplant himself into the existential situation from where he could speak of God, for he is unable to place himself into truth.

And so this unadulterated development of the transcendental thesis makes a stand against any objectivisation of God, whether this makes its appearance in the Catholic canonisation of history (the idea of the Church), in Protestant verbal inspiration or in the nineteenth-century theology of consciousness. God is not the God of our consciousness (Barth *contra* Schaeder); it is quite certain that a specific idea of God enters our consciousness when we speak of God, but it is no less certain that God himself is not thereby intercepted—inasmuch as we cannot speak of him at all as something there for the finding: on the contrary, only God himself can speak of God. To make God the content of my consciousness means to understand him as an entity. This has two consequences:

1. God "is" not, in the sense of an objecive entity; he is understanding himself in man within the act of faith; he is in the self-understanding of human existence within revelation. Whether he also "is" outside the act of faith, faith alone can say. The transcendental thesis leaves room for a being thus transcendent of the I, without (of course)

bringing it within reach of the I. For that reason faith may not be understood as essentially a psychic happening, though it is that too, but as the pure deed of God and of God alone.

2. If in this way God is apprehended as the subject of cognition, it is equally pressing, on one side, to understand the human I as subject of the knowledge of God (since otherwise the act of belief would have no contact with human existence) and, on the other side, to avoid identifying the human with the divine I. Thus one asks what mediation there is between the divine and the human acts of belief, what relation, in other words, subsists between grace and religion, revelation and history, with reference to the problem of knowledge.

This is the point where the profound difference between genuine transcendentalism and idealism stands clearly exposed. If in the latter (as has been shown, above) revelation was essentially religion through the identification of I and being, the original transcendental thesis marks a sharp contrast between the two. God " is " only in belief, but the subject of the believing is God himself. Hence faith is something essentially different from religion. But (even in Barth) no light is shed on how we can envisage the human religious act in conjunction with the divine act of belief, unless we sever them to allot them essentially different spheres, or suppress the " subjectivity " of God if not, alternatively, the existential impact of revelation. Religious acts of every kind may be stimulated by man, but only God himself can bestow faith, as full readiness to hear the Word; only he indeed can hear. The act of belief as reflected on cannot be distinguished from the religious act;

belief, because effected by God, is only in the act, never something left for the finding. But from that it follows that the I of belief, supposedly mine and God's together, can never be anything already present, but only something acting in the act of belief. Whether I do or do not believe is therefore something I cannot learn from any reflexion on my religious acts, but it is equally impossible, while I am in process of believing, to centre my attention on my belief in such a way that I would have to believe in my belief.[1] Belief is never directed to itself, but only on Christ, on something extrinsic. And so it is only in the believing in Christ that I know that I believe, which is to say that here and now I do not know it, and in reflexion on the believing I know nothing. From the non-objectivity of God follows necessarily the non-objectivity of whatever I knows God—but that implies the non-objectivity of faith.

If we were to discard this interpretation of revelation for another, the position could not but alter completely. However, such an exchange would only be possible if accompanied by a critique of the transcendental concept of knowledge which played so large a part in the purely act-centred theory of God's freedom and revelation. It was only within that epistemology that God's non-objectivity could be brought to clear philosophical expression and objectivity repudiated. Here some may disagree, but it may be that the concepts of objectivity and non-objectivity in the non-transcendental sense show themselves, in this context, inadequate to what they are called on to express.

[1] Even Luther could speak in these terms: W. A., 5, 164. Cf. O. Piper, *Theologie und reine Lehre*, 1926, p. 5.

Act and Being

Knowing and having: Through the act of knowing the known comes into the power of the I; it can be ranged within the system of general knowledge. *Qua* known, it " is " only in this system. The goal of cognition is to close this system. Once it succeeds, the I has become master of the world. For that reason alone, revelation is inimical to the system; for God is the master of the world, and the true system is an eschatological possibility. From that it seems an inescapable conclusion that God can be known only in the act, i.e. existentially. Otherwise he would deliver himself into the system. For knowing is having. Thus a chasm opens up between systematic and existential (*existentiell*) knowledge. Though the latter has in principle its place within thé former, as general knowledge it must sacrifice the cogency of the existential. This seems to be the only way in which God's claim to sole mastery can here be attested.

The world of my systematic knowledge remains in force even over the extent of my knowledge of God and fellow-man. Taking this standpoint, Bultmann is of the opinion that there can be talk of God " only as a kind of talk about ourselves " [1], since the " grasp of our existence " signifies " grasp of God ".[2] But here, at least in the formulation, he expresses a view which comes near to ignoring the fact that it is impossible for faith to be directed elsewhere than to God. It is speaking of God which first enables us to speak truly of ourselves. In reflexive theological thought I have no closer reference to my existence than to God.

[1] " Welchen Sinn hat es, von Gott zu reden? " in *Theologische Blätter*, 1925, No. 6, p. 133.
[2] Idem, p. 134.

On the contrary, one might paradoxically say that God is nearer to me than my existence is,[1] inasmuch as it is he who first discloses my existence to me. So there is no thoroughfare via " ourselves " to knowledge of God. It would therefore be impossible to speak of God or know (*wissen*) about God in a science (*Wissenschaft*) of theology unless it were incorrect to think of revelation as pure act, unless there were such a thing as a being of revelation outside my existential knowledge of it—outside my faith— on which my faith, my thought, my knowledge could "rest". Like transcendental philosophy, the theology evolved from the transcendental thesis is entangled in the peculiar reference of existence to transcendence. Its knowledge is implicated in the problem of existence. But a science (*Wissenschaft*), the essence of which is its knowing (*wissen*), not its asking, must be passionately interested in concepts of being; what *mode* of being is apposite here must remain for the present an unanswered question.

c. *Man and decision*

If existence is within truth only in the act of encounter with God, we may say that at a given time it has relapsed or is relapsing into untruth. Being unable, however, to place itself into truth, it " is " only in God's decision " for " it, which of course must also be understood as its decision for God. In other words, it " is " in its " having reference to God ", which rests on God's " having reference to the I ". Only existence standing in truth, i.e. in the decision, under- stands itself, and that in such a way that it knows itself

[1] Cf. Luther, W. A., 23, 135.

97

placed in truth by Christ, in judgment and mercy. Only at this point is it true to say " I am a sinner " or " I have been forgiven ". Outside the decision this may be a " known truth ", but not truth for me. And the recurrent lapse into untruth must be understood as decision against God, therefore as God's decision against me, his wrath against me. Thus declining to decide is already decision.

This is the consequence for the concept of existence, as it stands in the centre of dialectical theology, of interpreting revelation solely in terms of the act. " Whether we know it or not," [1] man is the question put to God, to which only God can give the answer. But this question, which we are, is not our destiny but our doing. " We ourselves are the accomplishers of our lives". [2] " Man's being is not conceived "—i.e. by St. Paul—" as a nature or substance, but accomplishes itself in its comportment towards God's claim, hence in its conduct, given that this is no process expending itself in time (like the working of a machine) but decision and responsible behaviour". [3]

[1] Bultmann, " Die Frage der dialektischen Theologie " in *Zwischen den Zeiten*, 1926, No. 1, p. 43.

[2] Barth, *Dogmatik*, I, p. 72.

[3] Bultmann in *Theologische Blätter*, 1928, No. 3, p. 66. Bultmann continues: " On that very account, he does not have power over his own being, since it is at stake in every Now, under the possibility, for Paul, of being determined by God or by sin". Here the concept of possibility is clearly suggested to Bultmann by Heidegger's Existential-ontological analysis of *Dasein* as the possibility of ontic existing. Consequently it includes the possibility of an ontological understanding of *Dasein* unaffected or unencountered by revelation. But, seen from the viewpoint of revelation, if " to be possible " means anything in reference to sin and grace (whether existentially or *existentiell*), it means to be already " in ", really in, one or the other. Here Bultmann differs very considerably from Barth, a point which has been demonstrated with

For man, to exist means to stand under God's claim, to conduct oneself, to make decisions. Existence is in pure *agere* (*Aktualität*). Consequently there is no self-understanding save in the act itself. There are no a priori concepts of existence (*keine Vorbegriffe über Existenz*). Man's existence is either in sin or in grace. Through (contingent) revelation there is only sinful existence or existence touched by grace: there is no potentiality.

In Bultmann's endeavour to use the historicity of existence as a basis for interpreting its instability (its invariably " being already guilty ") lurks the danger of a concept of existence achieved outside revelation. One can interpret the historicity of being from the position of sin, but not the state of sin from historicity.

In the indissoluble and exclusive reference of existence to revelation the original transcendental thesis comes into its own. The I is " with reference to " transcendence; it has instants of decision, but it decides in such a way that its decision is automatically a having-been-decided by the transcendental, just as the " with reference to transcendence " has as its basis the reference of (transcendent) being to *Dasein*. The problem here is how *Dasein qua* decision can be envisaged in continuity. This might appear simple if *Dasein* could be thought to decide over and over again for the " possibility most its own ", i.e. for sin, in which case this possibility is already reality. But even here we are still

---

absolute clarity by G. Kuhlmann, in the *Zeitschrift für Theologie und Kirsche*, 1929, No. 1. It need hardly be said that Bultmann is here no less widely separated from any understanding of act.

without indication of the light under which the being of sin can be understood as a whole. Still more does the new existence of faith appear to resist interpretation as a continuity of " being ". How are we to imagine a " *being* in faith ",[1] when the faith is an occasional, divinely effected decision? The requirement of continuity applies not only to the new existence as such but to the whole I as a unity, and to the empirical total I in general. The question is: how and with what right are we to think of existence, in particular the new existence, as a unified whole?

When we put the question of continuity, it becomes evident that Heidegger's concept of existence is useless for elucidating *being*-in-faith. Heidegger's *Dasein* is in continuity, since it is in the state of having relapsed to the world, in whose favour it has decided. Always *Dasein* finds itself already guilty[2]; it can summon itself back to itself out of the world, in conscience, but this possibility only confirms its perpetual condition. Now it is impossible to consider this already being in guilt as ontologically analogous to being in faith, because being as potentiality is confined within its own bounds, whereas faith is not in itself a human potentiality,[3] therefore not a being wherein existence finds

[1] English has *faith* and *belief* where German has only *Glaube*, but faith is already the being of belief. (*Translator*.)

[2] *Schuldig*, in Heidegger, expresses the existential-ontological, not the concrete Christian sense of the concept of guilt, therefore we cannot adopt it as the starting-point of our interpretation of " being " in sin. (It may be helpful to remember that *Schuld* has a basic sense of " owing ", " debt "—*Translator*.)

[3] Neither in the existential-ontological nor in the ontic sense: it is not any kind of possibility but a contingent advent of revelation in reality. Neither is sin a human potentiality, not even of fallen man, nor even an absolute possibility: it too is a happening reality.

itself as it attains itself. If understanding of being is regarded as an ontological characteristic of *Dasein*, we must with some dubiety ask whether and how the being of self-understanding existence is conceivable in the circumstances of an extrinsic revelation. It is unthinkable in the frame of Heidegger's *Existenz*, since this is confined within its existential-onto-logical possibilities. Yet only a being could under-lie the continuity of the new existence in unity with the I.

At this stage, further possible solutions are offered by attempts: 1. to preserve the continuity of the new existence at the expense of that of the total I (Barth); 2. to assert the continuity of the total I at the expense of that of the new existence (Bultmann).

1. In Barth we find the new I formally defined as the " non-being " of the old I. In any case the new I is at once " not-I ".[1] It is not intuitively evident; it is the suspension of the old I, and strictly imperceptible. It is " the non-being of the first world which is the being of the second, just as the second has its basis-of-being (*Seinsgrund*) in the non-being of the first ".[2] " The man to whom God reveals himself (*sich offenbart*) is the man to whom God cannot become man-ifest (*offenbar*). . . . He would have to conceive himself as not existing in order to conceive the Word of God coming to him. Properly understood, the position is that the man to whom God in reality reveals himself must see the revela-tion in this, his own impossibility".[3]

---

[1] Cf. *Römerbrief*, 3rd edition, especially pp. 125ff., 256ff.
[2] Op. cit., p. 142. (*Seinsgrund* may mean *raison d'être*, which would modify the apparent tautology—*Trans.*)
[3] *Dogmatik*, I, p. 287.

But the reason for Barth's statements lies in the fact that he can conceive revelation only as " non-revelation ". However, as the negation of the old man, the new man can in fact be understood in continuity of the I. Yet two considerations remain:

(*a*) Are we to think of the new I in unity with the empirical total I, or does it remain the latter's " heavenly double "? This is a question which puts Barth's concept of the act on trial. If the act of the new I has a supratemporal continuity, the danger of empirical theology is wholly averted—but at the expense of man's historicity, hence existential act-character. As absolutely supratemporal the act of the new I (=act of the Holy Spirit) must be regarded as the horizontal, as well as the infinitude of the vertical, whence we may more easily understand Barth's characteristic wavering between use and rejection of temporal definitions of the act of belief.[1] In essence, the eternal act always " precedes " " any " historical act: in fact, because it is free; logically, because for that very reason conceived in pure negation. Barth is well aware that he has to define the total I as historical, yet his concepts have already been over-defined before he approaches that of the historical. When he comes to it, he doubtless says everything that needs to be said, but he has unfortunately said too many things beforehand. Consequently he can no longer render the I comprehensible as a historical total I. As against this we maintain that the essence of the *actus directus* does not lie in its timelessness but in its intentionality towards

[1] See p. 82 above, with preceding quotations, and cf. Barth's " Bemerkungen zu H. M. Müller's *Lutherbuch* " in *Zwischen den Zeiten*, 1929, No. 6.

Christ, which is not repeatable at will, because it is freely given by God. This is as much as to say that its essence is expressed by its manner of touching upon existence—by which we mean the totality of historical, temporal *Existenz*. For this reason alone it is not amenable to demonstrative " heres and theres ", even if it does fulfil itself in the concrete, conscious, psychic event whose material may be reproduced and submitted to reflexion. This is a valid application of the proposition (see p. 12 above) that the *actus directus* may offer material to reflexion, though in its pure intentionality —here founded in and directed on Christ—it does not enter reflexion at all.

(*b*) If I and not-I are envisaged in the relation of inter-negation, the belief of the I must be directed towards its identity with not-I. But this forces the act of belief into a crooked path. Belief knows only an " outward " direction, to cross and resurrection, and knows itself, as an act of the empirical total I, to be critically affected with it by those events. It is in this sense that dogmatics has to grasp the problem of continuity. For Barth there would also be the question of how the believing I, which as believing is already not-I, could still believe in this not-I, or whether there are two distinct acts of belief, one of the I and another of the not-I. In this way the problem is once more reduced to that of the *actus directus*.[1]

---

[1] Naturally one cannot fail to see that Barth himself tries his utmost to insist that faith can only believe in God; it is on this very point that the dialectical method of discussing God hinges. Notwithstanding, there is still an essential difference between my asking, in faith, about my identity with myself and my asking about the grace of God in which this identity must have its basis. Of its nature, belief can no longer call itself in question, since it has a basis of unity, though

2. Bultmann's concept of historicity enables him to imagine the continuity of the new I with the total I.[1] The whole I stands under God's claim: in decision for God it becomes the new I *in toto*, in relapse to sin the old I. Always it is entirely itself. " We are always on trial, to see how we will seize the possibilities of our historical existence; since the historical fact of Jesus Christ, to see whether we want to belong to God or to the Devil." [2] The Word of forgiveness points our way into historicity.[3] So far, so good. But how can we now envisage the new I in continuity? Is being in Christ constituted only by every conscious act of decision for Christ? And what in this case *is* decision? What is the meaning of " *wanting* " to belong to God or to the Devil? Clearly a decision by God is postulated, for this decision is neither an *existentiell* nor existential possibility of my existence. As I find myself already in guilt, so as a believer I would have to find myself already in Christ. But it is not at all clear how " I ", being already in guilt, can be thought of as now in Christ. It would appear to depend on the possibility of somehow bringing this being of the new I into conjunction with the concept of existence, unless we are to assume a discontinuous new I.[4] To us,

---

unbelief can doubt Christ and thus import reflexion into the act of belief. But this distinction has decisive consequences for the concept of existence.

[1] Cf. *Theologische Blätter*, 1928, No. 3, pp. 65f.

[2] Bultmann, " Zur Frage der Christilogie " in *Zwischen den Zeiten*, 1928, pp. 67f.

[3] *Theologische Blätter*, 1928, No. 3.

[4] Even supposing the possibility of an existential-ontological unity of existence, an account would still be lacking of what is meant by " being in Christ ".

however, that possibility appears to require the idea of the Church for its realisation.

It is R. Seeberg who here provides a positive view, evolved in connection with his Lutheran studies. From the standpoint of his logical voluntarism he introduces the concept of the new direction of will. In this he veers from the genuinely transcendental thesis towards idealism. The new I is the new will, which God has turned into the direction which points to him, and which, being now in the right direction, does good of its own accord. Thereby the historicity of the I, the continuity of the total I with the new I, and the continuity of the new I itself are preserved. The problem of *everydayness* seems to be satisfactorily solved by the concept of direction. " Being in Christ " means the possession of the new direction of will. The interpretations of revelation in terms of act and of being are genuinely combined. One must first digest the manifest simplicity of the conception before proceeding to a few questions. These arise in the first place from Seeberg's concept of sin. The justified man remains a sinner. What can that mean in Seeberg's theory save that the wrong direction is still a constituent of the justified man? If accordingly the new direction must be regarded not as continuous but as interrupted by the old, what are we to think of the continuity of the total I?

Secondly, is there a will not consciously aiming at God, which might be claimed as the will of the justified man? Is the everyday direction of the will really direction to God? Unless this be so, we are left with a new I that

recurrently perishes and revives. Once again we should
have to look elsewhere for continuous being. Because
the new direction must be sought or given in each discrete
act, it seems impossible to form any answer to our
question.

Again, the concept of direction does not guarantee the
unity of the concept of the person. As a factor of no more
than psychological standing, direction is subject to dissection
into individual acts and whatever interpretation may be
imposed. Here Seeberg gives occasion to revive the objec-
tions propounded by Luther in his momentous exposure
of nominalism: man must be conceived as a unity before
we can set him over against the oneness of God. This unity,
however, is something which a psychological concept, as
such, is unable to convey: even according to Luther, man
is self-impenetrable in his psychology. Nobody knows his
own motives, nobody wholly knows his own sin; man is
unable to understand himself from his own psychical
experiences; they are susceptible of every arbitrary interpretation. Be that as it may, since, as was shown above,
there is human self-understanding only—if at all—from the
oneness of man, and since the understanding of man supposes
a potential reproduction, the unity must be sought where
man is created or re-created and this being-created is
executed " on " him yet also with him—where man must
know himself, without interpretation, in utter clarity and
reality. But this is to say that the unity of man, of human
existence, is founded solely in the Word of God. This
Word permits man to understand himself as " being in
Adam " or " being in Christ ", " being in the communion

of Christ ", in such a way that the fact of the unity's basis in the Word is identical with the fact of its basis in being in Adam or Christ.   Now this is not an empirical datum but is given to faith as revelation.   Only in faith is the unity, the " being ", of the person disclosed.

2

REVELATION IN TERMS OF BEING

A. *The " being " of revelation*

Unmistakably, *agere sequitur esse*, the basic ontological thesis of Catholic and traditional Protestant dogmatics, expresses the antithesis of transcendentalism. It is the *esse* which we have to interpret; the business of ontological analysis is to understand the continuity of man and revelation. It has to establish of revelation that God " is " in it, and of man that he " is " before he acts, and acts only out of that " being ". The ontological account of the being of revelation defines it as, in principle, transcending consciousness and " objective ": it can somehow be brought to givenness, it exists, is there, present, accessible, in being; it is independent of the consciousness, does not fall into its power. Within ontology itself, this definition is open to divers readings.

In complete contrast to the transcendental endeavour, three possibilities are available from the outset to the explanation of revelation in terms of being. Revelation is understood: 1. as doctrine [1]; 2. as psychic experience; 3. as an institution.

1. If the essence of revelation is taken to be doctrine,

[1] Or " theory ", " lore " (*Lehre*)—*Translator.*

108

then its explanation will follow in terms of ontological concepts, for doctrine is basically continuous and accessible —hence can be freely accepted or rejected. If God binds himself within a doctrine of his nature, he may be found in that doctrine, understood and allocated his place in human " existence ". But this leaves the existence of man un-affected, unencountered. Even a doctrine of the merciful God, even one which states that wherever man and God come together, there the Cross must stand—even such a doctrine is in itself no stumbling-block (at least to our modern way of thinking), but rather a wholly welcome addition to our " system ". The stumbling-block, the scandal, arises only when our existence is really affected, when we not only hear of the Cross and judgment but, hearing, needs must deliver ourselves to them, that grace may descend. If, then, it is only a divinely created faith which can appropriate the doctrine, it is clear that to revelation *qua* doctrine is added some other constituent which in one way or another exceeds the ontological possibilities of man. From this it follows that when revela-tion is understood *only* as doctrine, the Christian idea of revelation eludes the grasp, because there has been an attempt to seize God with an ontological apparatus which is adequate only to the human.

2. If we here revert to the attempt to understand revela-tion as an experience in consciousness, the justification is that we now see another aspect of the fusing of act- and being-concepts which was demonstrated above in respect of idealism. The " objectivity " of the entity is conferred on revelation once it is understood as religious experience. God is then present in my experience, understandable,

amenable to classification in the human system of experiences. Thus here, too, existence goes unaffected. But in understanding revelation it is not a question of reproducing this or that experience—in principle, any experience, even if religious, is reproducible—but of knowing that revelation has impinged upon my existence, disclosing it and transplanting it into a new manner of existing. Again, therefore, the reference is to something else which lies beyond revelation *qua* experience, from which it follows that to understand revelation in this sense is to overlook the decisive factor. From this point of view it is likewise impossible to understand the being of the new man, since existence is unaffected.

3. If former attempts ended by delivering revelation into the power of the human subject, the last possibility of grasping the being of revelation trans-subjectively appears to consist in conceiving it as a divine institution—a view to which the Catholic Church adheres, as well as Protestant orthodoxy with its assertion of the Bible's verbal inspiration. In the institution God " is " as one directly confined and at the disposal of man. Catholicism takes this to mean that whoever is in the institution is in God. Yet the being of man is located wholly in the trans-subjective. Correspondingly the grace infused into him through the Church is represented from the outset as a kind of " being ", in the form of a habitus (*habitus entitativus!*). The stress is laid entirely on the being of man. That his substance should remain untouched by the accidental quality of grace opens a problem unsuitable for discussion here,[1] but it goes to

[1] On how far the substance *is* affected, cf. Bartmann, *Lehrbuch der Dogmatik*, II, pp. 101f., including his quotations from Aquinas.

show that even here the existence of man is unaffected. His being is said to have its foundation in the trans-subjective, for there can be impact on his existence only "from outside"; therefore the new being must be founded and sustained from outside, and the sacrament of ordination—which is basic to the Catholic idea of Church—stands warranty for that. To the stipulation of the " from outside ", however, should be added this other, no less indispensable, that it must be truly the whole existence of man which is transplanted into a new manner of being; otherwise even the " outside " is no genuine " outside ", for it is defined as such by the fact of coming from the farther side of all intra-existential possibilities to impinge on existence itself and create it anew. This, though, is not guaranteed in the Catholic ontology of revelation. The being of an institution is incapable of affecting the existence of man *qua* sin; it cannot stand over against man, be ob-jective (*gegen-ständlich*) in the full sense. That is only possible in the real meeting with another person; from this we see that although on the one hand it is correct to make the transition from the ontology of revelation to the concept of the Church, on the other hand the Church should here be conceived not in an institutional sense but in terms of persons. Thus we are re-directed into the path earlier forecast.

The reason why these three ways of explaining revelation in terms of being are inadequate to the Christian idea of revelation is this: they understand the revealed God as an entity, whereas entities are transcended by act and being. Man assimilates them into his transcendental I, and so they are unable to be ob-jective in the full sense, hence are useless for theological explanation of the revelation in Christ which bears against Adam's very manner of existence. The entity, that is to say, or the creaturely, cannot shake the existence of man—not even in the " Thou ", the " claim of my neighbour " (Gogarten, Grisebach)—unless God himself assail and turn man from his ways. That this happens " through " entity is the problem of revelation, but everything depends on the interpretation of " through ".

There is no hiding the fact that the identification of entity and revelation failed to make articulate any genuine ontology. It arose on that frontier of thought where the compulsion of inner logic broke down and the paths of transcendentalism and ontology diverged, the latter suspending thought itself in being, which therefore also transcended the entity. Yet in principle the being of the entity is demonstrable *in* the entity, hence ob-jective for demonstrative indication (*Aufweis*) or for intuitive perception (*für das Schauen*). Here the crucial problem of critical ontology is how the " indicated " being is to be thought of in distinction from the entity. The critical suspension of thought in being is the only way of preserving the basic thesis at all, but even this admits of differing courses (consider Heidegger for example, who from this position arrives at the idealistic system).

Indicated being is still, of course, being in the manner of entities (*seiendes Sein*), but that raises no difficulty for ontological thought, since it has a different reason from the Kantian for the transcending of the entity; whereas transcendentalism holds the entity, *qua* objective, to be conditioned by the act, hence transcended by the non-objective, ontology thinks it only through the entity that being can be brought to pure demonstration, final givenness. Thus for the pure ontology of revelation it is as wrong to volatilise revelation into non-entity as to treat it wholly as entity. It must rather be thought of as enjoying a mode of being which embraces both entity and non-entity, while at the same time " suspending " within itself man's intention of it—faith.

B. *The knowledge of revelation*

If revelation is an object of knowledge *qua* entity, it follows that there must be a direct positive knowledge. The system rises up on firm ground as the in-itself adequate knowledge of revelation. To this concept of revelation as an object there would correspond the phenomenological method, for which " entitative " revelation would represent the supra-formal, substantive a priori of cognition (i.e. here, of faith). But the phenomenological method is carried out within the existence of man; for man must already bear within him the potentialities of essential vision—i.e. here, the knowledge of revelation—and can " lay bare " the being behind the entity because deep within him he already knows what " being " is. From that it follows, however, that pheno-menology must fail to understand Christian revelation, which it thus regards as an entity in the sense of something not contingent, but there for the finding. Human existence itself cannot be approached via such entities, whether they are interpreted transcendentally or onto-phenomenologi-cally.

And so a *genuine* ontology of revelation demands a concept of knowledge which involves the existence of man without languishing in utter act-subjectivism, and a cognitive object (*Gegenstand*) which in the full sense " stands over against " (*entgegensteht*) the I. This means that the object, firstly, must challenge and constrain the I's manner of existence— without, that is, submitting, like the spuriously objective entity, to transcendence by act or being. Secondly, it must in principle be independent of its being known; finally, it must confront the I in such a way that man's very knowing is based on and suspended in a being-already-known. The *Gegenstand* must at all times already *entgegenstehen*; it may be an entity only in the non-committal sense of being rather than not being. As such it must be an " entity " whose being and existence underlie or precede those of the I, one to which cognition cannot however have recourse at will, as if to something there for its finding, but in the presence of which it must always itself be suspended in cognition.

Then indeed the revelation preached to us of God in Christ, the three-in-one person self-bestowed on us, would be the object of our knowing.

c. *Man as " being in . . ."*

The conception of revelation as an entity would have the following result for man's stock of knowledge, that he could freely and constantly recur to this entity, which is there for the finding. It stands at his disposal, whether it be religious experience, the verbally inspired Bible or the Catholic Church. He knows himself assured by this entity, borne up by this entity—though this assurance can only consist in the fact that man remains by himself, since, as we have seen, the entity as such is finally given into his power. And so the I allots the entity a place of precedence over itself, freely subordinates itself to it with *fides implicita*—though this, again, it can only do because it thus feels a final self-assurance, because it is thus enabled to remain by itself, because therefore the entity is still subordinate to the I!—and finds itself under the protection of this entity. It can never stray from the protective " area of jurisdiction " of the verbally inspired Bible, the factuality, etc., of religious experience; it is " in " the institutional Catholic Church. Yet, as entity, none of this can have impact on existence in the way we have defined.

Indeed, only one kind of knowledge is compatible with this definition, a kind which is also demanded by the true ontology of revelation: knowledge that the existence of man is invariably a " being in . . .". This " being in . . .", however, must satisfy two all-important requirements: 1. it must involve the existence of man; 2. it must be possible to think of the being in continuity. If we add that the reality of revelation is that very being, taking on the mode of entity (*das seiende Sein*), which constitutes the being (the existence) of man, but that this being is the divine person, our picture is complete—provided that this is understood as " being in Christ ", i.e. " being in the " Church ". But since this being must affect the very existence of man, there must be existential acts which accompany it and constitute it as much as they are constituted by it.

This is where a *genuine* ontology comes into its own, inasmuch as it defines the " being in . . ." in such a way that cognition, finding itself in the world of entity, suspends

115

itself when confronted by the being of the entity and does not force it under its control.

It is from this position that it becomes permissible to speak theologically about the nature of man, his knowledge of God, God's knowledge of him. From here opens the prospect of genuine theological concepts of being.

3

THE CHURCH AS A UNITY
OF ACT AND BEING

First, a survey of the important questions raised:

1. Whence do I acquire understanding of existence (*Dasein*), of myself? It has already been shown that the existence of man can only be radically affected from outside and understands itself only in being thus encountered. There is no true " from outside " save in revelation.

2. How are we to think of revelation's mode of being, actwise or ontologically? What is meant by the freedom of God? What theological account can we give of the " being " of God in revelation?

3. How are we to think of man's mode of being? As decision or as " being in . . ."? How can the continuity of the I be affirmed?

4. What results from either analysis of revelation for the concept of knowledge, i.e. for man's cognition of God, positive theological knowledge (*Wissen*), the concept of science (*Wissenschaft*), the system?

In what follows an endeavour will be made to treat these questions in terms of the concept Church and to answer them from the position gained. Accordingly we have the following heads of discussion: 1. the Church as the centre of the understanding of existence; 2. the mode of being, within the Church, of the revelation of God; 3. man's mode of being within the Church; 4. the problem of knowledge within the Church.

A. *The Church as the place where* Dasein *is understood*

The foregoing discussion has all been directed to or determined by one focus, which up to now has remained imperfectly visible. The discussion cannot, in fact, be fully understood until brought into the light shed by the idea of the Church; it is not really meaningful to assert that any attempt at an autonomous understanding of *Dasein* must fail a priori, unless we stand on premises which deny *Dasein* the possibility of placing itself into truth. These premises themselves are not possible from within *Dasein* (hence not doctrine, experience, institution), but represent a contingent event, truly " from outside ", which has bound us to itself and by placing us in truth has bestowed on us understanding of *Dasein*. In any philosophy of merely existential possibilities there can be no place for the contingency of this event of revelation in the Christian Church, in Cross and resurrection, otherwise it would not be a contingency in the fullest sense, not revelation, not an event of divine provenance for the atonement of *sinful* humanity. Only one who stands on these premises must condemn as untruth the attempts of *Dasein* to understand itself out of its own possibilities. But if it is a deed of God which involves man in the event called revelation, this lies outside the possibilities of any autonomous philosophy of *Dasein*, which implies that

118

the premises can be justified by nothing less than God—or the event itself.

The time has come to define these premises more closely. Man's being involved in the event called revelation must here be conceived as being in the Church, i.e. as a theo-sociological category, and from this viewpoint the questions raised must then be discussed and answered in connection with the problem of act and being.

B. *Revelation's mode of being within the Church*

Revelation should be envisaged only with reference to the Church, where the Church is regarded as constituted by the present annunciation, within the communion, for the communion, of Christ's death and resurrection. " Present ", because it is only in this annunciation that the event of revelation is realised in and for the communion and because, secondly, this is the only way in which its contingent (i.e. extrinsic) character makes itself known—for contingency is only in presence, viz. the present. What is past, as "having" happened, is " background ", unless the annunciation " coming to " us in the future should raise it to " presence ".[1] In the concept of contingency as happening which is " coming to " us from outside, the present is determined by the future; in the system, inasmuch as the (in principle) " beforeness " of the rational background obtains, the present is determined by the past. At all events the present

[1] Bonhoeffer stresses the literal sense of *Zukunft* (" future ")—" to-coming ". German *Gegenwart*, it may be remarked, means " the present " and " presence " alike. " Communion " here means the spiritual Christian community, never the Eucharist. (*Translator.*)

is determined by one or the other or both; it is never *per se.*
But the decision lies with man. Of the Christian revelation
it may be said that the annunciation of Cross and resurrection, determined by eschatology and predestination, together
with the event effective within it, serves even to raise the
past to the present and, paradoxically, to something future,
yet " to come ". It follows, therefore, that we may not
interpret the Christian revelation as " having happened ",
that for man living in the Church, in the present, this unique
occurrence is qualified as future.[1] Conversely, for the very
reason that the Christian revelation, in its special qualifica-
tion of the unique event of Cross and resurrection, is always
" yet to come ", it must happen in the present: that is to
say, it must be considered within the Church, for the
Church is the Christ of the present, " Christ existing as
community ". In the annunciation within the communion
for the communion, Christ is the " subject " common to
annunciation (Word and sacrament) and communion alike.
The annunciation and the communion are so interdependent
that each, regarded for itself alone, loses its meaning altogether. Christ is the corporate person of the Christian
communion: see especially I Cor. 12, 12; 6, 15; 1, 13;
Rom. 6, 13 and 19; Eph. 2, 14. The Church is the body
of Christ: I Cor. 12, 12ff.; Rom. 12, 4ff.; Eph. 1, 23;
4, 15f.; Col. 1, 18. Christ is in the communion as the
communion is in Christ: I Cor. 1, 30; 3, 16; II Cor. 6, 16;
13, 5; Col. 2, 17; 3, 11. The communion is a corporate
person whose name is also Christ: Gal. 3, 28; Col. 3, 10f.;

---

[1] This could be the starting-point for a philosophy of time peculiarly
Christian in comparison with the concept of time as something reckoned
by physical motion.

cf. Eph. 1, 23. Note also the expression " put on the new man ", which sometimes takes the form, " put on the Lord Jesus ": Col. 3, 10; Eph. 4, 24; Rom. 13, 14; Gal. 3, 27.[1]

This is why the Protestant idea of the Church is conceived in personal terms, *scil.* God reveals himself as a person in the Church. The Christian communion is God's final revelation: God as " Christ existing as community ", ordained for the rest of time until the end of the world and the return of Christ.[2] It is here that Christ has come the very nearest to humanity, here given himself to his new humanity, so that his person enfolds in itself all whom he has won, binding itself in duty to them, and them reciprocally in duty to him. The " Church " therefore has not the meaning of a human community to which Christ is or is not self-superadded, nor of a union among such as individually seek or think to have Christ and wish to cultivate this common " possession "; no, it is a communion created by Christ and founded upon him, one in which Christ reveals himself as the δεύτερος ἄνθρωπος, the new man—or rather, the new humanity itself.

This is where the question of explaining revelation in terms of act or being assumes an entirely new aspect. God gives himself in Christ to his communion, and to each

[1] Cf. also Kattenbusch, " Quellort der Kirchenidee ", in the *Festgabe* to Harnack, 1921, pp. 143ff., and Traugott Schmidt, *Der Leib Christi.* See further Scheler's theory of corporate persons in *Der Formalismus in der Ethik und die materiale Wertethik.* In my *Sanctorum communio: eine dogmatische Untersuchung zur Soziologie der Kirche*, 1930 (new edition 1954), I sought to apply this idea in the dogmatic field.

[2] The tension between " Christ existing as community " and the heavenly Christ whom we await—persists.

individual as member of that communion. This he does in such a way that the active subject in the communion, of both the annunciation and the believing of the Word, is Christ. It is in the personal communion, and only there, that the gospel can truly be declared and believed. There, it follows, revelation is in some way secured or possessed. God's freedom has bound itself, woven itself into the personal communion, and it is precisely that which proves it God's freedom—that he should bind himself to men. The communion genuinely has at its disposal the Word of forgiveness; in the communion may not only be said, existentially, " I have been forgiven ", but also—by the Christian Church as such, in preaching and sacrament—" thou art forgiven "; furthermore, every member of the Church may and should " become a Christ " to every other in so proclaiming the gospel.

Revelation, then, happens within the communion; it demands primarily a Christian sociology of its own. The distinction between thinking of revelation individualistically and thinking of it in relation to community is fundamental. All the problematics we have examined so far have had an individualistic orientation. Both the transcendental essay at act-subjectivism and the ontological attempt to establish the continuity of the I envisaged consistently the individual man, and he was the rock on which they both foundered. They overlooked, in searching for " reality ", that man in reality is never *only* the single unit, not even the *one* "claimed by the Thou", but invariably finds himself in some community, whether in " Adam " or in " Christ ". The Word of God is given to mankind, the gospel to the communion of Christ. When the sociological category is thus introduced, the problem of act and being—and also the problem of knowledge—is presented in a wholly fresh light.

The being of revelation does not lie in a unique occurrence of the past, in an entity which in principle is at my disposal and has no direct connection with my old or my new existence, neither can the being of revelation be conceived solely as the ever-free, pure and non-objective act which at certain times impinges on the existence of individuals. No, the being of revelation " is " the being of the community of persons, constituted and embraced by the person of Christ, wherein the individual finds himself to be already in his new existence. This ensures three considerations: 1. the being of revelation can be envisaged in continuity; 2. the existence of man is critically involved; 3. it is impossible to regard the being of revelation as entity, as objective, or on the other hand as non-entity, as non-objective.

1. The continuity of revelation means that it is constantly present (in the sense of the *futurum*, the yet " to come "). To-day, therefore, it can only be a question of the Christ preached in the Church, his death and resurrection. If the individual as such were the hearer of the preaching, the continuity would still be endangered, but it is the Church itself which hears the Church's Word, even if " I " were heedless on such and such an occasion. Thus preaching is always heard. It is outside " me " that the gospel is proclaimed and heard, that Christ " is " in his community. And so it is not in man that the continuity lies: it is suprapersonally guaranteed through a community of persons. Instead of the institutional Catholic Church we have the community as the trans-subjective pledge of revelation's

continuity and extrinsicality—the "from outside" (cf. point 3, below).

2. But the existence of the individual man, hearing the Word on concrete occasions, is vitally affected by this community, inasmuch as, drawn into it, he finds himself already there and as one placed into the truth of his old and new existence. This fact derives from the personal quality of the Christian communion, in that its subject is Christ. For only through persons, and only through the person of Christ can the existence of man be affected, placed into truth and transplanted into a new manner of existing. Since moreover the person of Christ has revealed itself in the communion, the existence of man can only be so affected through the communion. It is only from the person of Christ that other persons acquire for man the character of personhood. In this way they even become Christ for us in what they both demand and promise, in their existential impositions upon us from without. At the same time they become, as such, the pledge of revelation's continuity. If the existence of man were unaffected by revelation within the communion, all we have said about the being of revelation in the communion would be pointless. Continuity which does not also impinge on existence is not the continuity of the Christian revelation, not present being, but bygone entity. In other words, the communion guarantees the continuity of revelation only by the fact that I know and believe myself to be in this communion. Here the problem of act and being receives its final clarification by taking the shape of the dialectic of faith and Church. But of that, later.

3. If the being of revelation is fixed in entity, it remains

past, existentially impotent; if it is volatilised into the non-objective, its continuity is lost. And so the being of revelation must enjoy a mode of being which satisfies both claims, embodying both the continuity proper to being and the existential significance of the act. It is as such a mode of being that we understand the person and the community. Here the possibility of existential impact is bound up with genuine objectivity in the sense of a concrete standing-over-against: this lets itself be drawn into the power of the I because it itself imposes a constraint on existence, because it is *the* extrinsicality.

The community in question is concretely visible, is the Christian Church which hears and believes the preaching of the Word. The Word of this community is preaching and sacrament, its conduct is believing and loving. It is in this concretion that one must think of the being of revelation, in " Christ existing as community ". Only thus, in the concretion of the mode of being of a true (i.e. Christ-founded) community of persons, can one observe and preserve the hovering between entity and non-entity.

Qua extrinsicality the personal revelation presents itself in correlation with my whole existence, i.e. in a sociological category. It is essentially distinct from the category of " there is ".[1] " There is " is existentially indifferent. It belongs with individualistic, epistemological thought in terms of " things". Revelation's mode of being, on the other hand, is definable only with reference to persons.

[1] It may be worth remarking that the German *es gibt* is more firmly linked than " there is " with notions of " the given ", the available, hence dominable, manipulable—*Translator.*

" There is " only the entity, the given. It is self-contradictory to seek a " there is " on the farther side of entity.
In the social context of the person the static ontology of
" there is " is set in motion. There is no God that " there
is ". God " is " in the personal reference, and (?his) being
is his being a person (*und das Sein ist sein Personsein*).

Of course that is only comprehensible to the man who
is placed in truth, the man for whom, through the person
of Christ, his neighbour has become genuinely a person.
For the man in untruth revelation remains, as " person "
remains, an entity or thing which " there is ": towards
this one's relation and attitude are neutral in the sense that
the existence of man is not critically involved. It is only
within the communion itself that revelation can be conceived
in its real existential being. And so we come to require an
account of the being of man in revelation.

c. *Man's mode of being within the Church*

*Prius est enim esse quam operari, prius autem pati quam esse. Ergo
fieri, esse, operari se sequuntur.*[2] In relation to God man has
the passive position, is a " sufferer ": Luther is speaking
of the *nova nativitas.* Existence is defined as *pati;* " authen-
tically ", that is to say, one can speak of existence only as
of existence which undergoes, hence any concept of existence
which ignores impact from without (as by Christ) or the
absence of such impact is " inauthentic " (including
Heidegger's " authentic " existence). Earlier we made this

[2] *Röm.-Br.*, Komm. ed. F. Ficker, I, 110, 26ff.; cf. also the Notice
and II, 266, 10ff., and the relevant literature mentioned in the Notice.
E. Seeberg, *Luthers Theologie*, I, p. 67.

concept of existence into a critical yardstick against which any other must fail. Existence in this sense is existence in social context with reference to Christ, knowing itself accepted or rejected. Existence, therefore, is only as sinful and as forgiven. If we are to discover how human existence, as *pati*, in the communion of Christ is related to the problem of act and being, or how the concept of *pati* includes existentiality and continuity, we must look to the concept of the Church.

1. To " become " a member of Christ's Church man must believe (it being understood that this is not a human possibility, since faith is given by God). It is only in such faith that man " has " God. And according to the measure of his faith man has much, little or nothing of God. To that it would appear to correspond, conversely, that God " is " only in faith, is not where he is not believed. This conception, of which the first aspect is not infrequent in Luther,[1] has been introduced by R. Seeberg into his system as religious transcendentalism.[2] There is no salvation except in faith, no " being " of atonement, as an ascertainable entity in Church, doctrine, etc., save in connection with the I in existential acts. There is a " being " of revelation only in faith *qua* act of belief. Here the *sola fide* seems preserved at its purest.

2. Faith has being in the Church as its condition. Faith invariably discovers itself already in the Church. When it comes to know that it is in the Church, it was already there. To believe is as much as to say: to find God, his grace and

[1] W. A., 3, 523; 40, 1, 360; 40, 2, 342f.; quoted in the Lutheran studies of R. and E. Seeberg.
[2] Cf. p. 44 above.

the community of Christ already present. Faith encounters a being which is prior to the act; it depends on this being, because it knows itself involved in it as a special declension of it. The being is not dependent on the faith; on the contrary, the faith knows that the being is wholly independent of itself, of its own being or non-being. All hangs on this: that it knows itself not as somehow conditioning or even creating, but as conditioned by, created by, this being.

3. The being of revelation, the Christ-communion, is only in faith. Faith knows that revelation is independent of it. These two propositions must combine to make a third: only in faith does man know that the being of revelation, his own being in the Church of Christ, is independent of faith. There is continuity of revelation, continuity of existence, only in faith, but there again in such a way that faith *qua* believing is suspended only in " faith " *qua* " being in the communion ". If here faith were understood wholly as an act, the continuity of being would be disrupted by the discontinuity of acts. Since however faith as an act knows itself as the mode of being of its being in the Church, the continuity is indeed only " in the believing " but thereby is really preserved as being in the Church.

From this point of view it seems possible to combine in reciprocal complementation two views so opposed as that of Flacius, with his *perpetua justificatio*, and that of the Calvinist Zanchi, with his *perseverantia sanctorum*. Whereas according to the former's doctrine of man as *imago Satanae* the *justificatio* could never become a " being " of man but must be re-created in separate acts, Zanchi claimed knowledge of a being of man, based on predestination, which can no more be affected by acts than vanish altogether: what God has chosen is chosen for eternity. Both ignored the central significance of the idea of the Church. Flacius could scarcely have failed to see, from the standpoint of that idea, that his concept of faith is individualistic and inadequate, that individual acts of faith are already within a being in the communion of Christ. Zanchi likewise would have recognised that the act of faith alone can penetrate to the being, which here is no entity ready for the finding, no " there is ", but one to be known and known again in the act, one that understands itself in the act and whose continuity and genuine extrinsicality can be asserted only in this understanding. Predestination as a doctrine (seeing that it comes under consideration, for faith, only in the historical revelation in Christ) produces concepts of being which, to the extent that man has at his command, for ready reference, the divine knowledge of his own predestination,[1] assume the form of entity, whereas concepts of being derived from the idea of the Church are always formed with reference to the act of faith. Zanchi was undoubtedly right to wish to express the continuity of the divine activity at work upon man, hence of man's new being, but Flacius is no less justified in demanding a *perpetua justificatio*, for he thereby guards against an ontology seeking to understand the being of the new man as an implanted psychic habitus, therefore entity, against which Flacius correctly recognises

[1] Barth takes a different view, regarding predestination as the mystery which lies before and behind everything; this renders a " being " impossible.

that the act of faith is in one way or another an essential component of the being of the new man; however, for Flacius faith remains an actual constituent of that new being, rather than its correlative *manner* of being.

4. It is through the sociological category that the dialectic of faith and " being in . . ." in the concept of man finds its concrete interpretation, which will be argued more explicitly in Part Three.

In accordance with the being of revelation, the being of man should be conceived neither frozen as entity nor spirited into non-entity. In either of these cases the total existence of man would, in the end, stay unaffected. No; the man we must consider is the historical man who knows himself transplanted from the old into the new humanity and who is, by membership of the new, a person re-created by Christ, a person who " is " only in the act-reference to Christ and whose being " with reference to " Christ is based on being in Christ and his communion in such a way that the act is " suspended " in the being, while the being itself " is " not in the absence of the act. The person, as a synthesis of act and being, is always two in one: *individual* and *humanity*. The concept of the absolute individual is an abstraction with no corresponding reality. It is not merely in his general psychology but in his very existentiality that man is tied to society. When his existence is touched (in judgment and mercy) he knows that he is being directed towards humanity. He has himself committed the sin of the old humanity, yet he knows at the same time that humanity drew him into its sin and guilt when he was powerless to resist. He is the bearer of the new humanity in his faith, prayer and affirmation, yet knows that he is borne in all his actions by the communion, by Christ.[1]

Man as individual and man as humanity, man one in these two inseparable aspects, is but another way of saying man as act and being. He is never one alone. It might be supposed that man's humanity-being could be understood as an abstraction without the slightest effect on existence, but such a supposition collapses against the historical reality of Christ's communion and my membership thereof. In *reality* I hear another man declare the gospel to me, see him offer me the sacrament: " thou art forgiven ", see and hear him and the congregation praying for me; at the same time *I* hear the gospel, I join in the prayer and I know myself joined into the Word, sacrament and prayer of the communion of Christ, the new humanity now as then, here as elsewhere; I bear it upon me and am borne of it. Here I, the historically whole man, individual and humanity together, am encountered, affected. I believe; that is, I know myself borne: I am borne (*pati*), therefore I am (*esse*), therefore I believe (*agere*). The circle closes. For even *agere* is *pati* here; but the I always remains the historical One—though in faith the New One. Needless to say, *as* historical it is a member of the new humanity which " here " or " there " takes the shape of empirical communities of individuals—though retaining the mode of being of revelation.

Is not the continuity of the I destroyed by the fact that the I, as historical, falls apart into religious life and profane life? What are we to make of the fact of everydayness? Even if

[1] Cf. especially Luther's Sermon on the Holy Body of Christ, 1519. See also what is said below on being in Adam or in Christ.

we refrain from describing historicity, everydayness, as a divine punishment, the difficulty obtains only from a standpoint of unbelieving reflexion. Religious acts are simply not identical with faith, otherwise the being of faith would once again be explicable as " entity ". The unity of the I " is " " only in faith ". Everything points to that conclusion. If it were possible for unbelief to discover being in continuity (e.g. as everyday psychical datum), the evangelical understanding of faith would be at fault and being would be entity.

But what is meant by the unity of the historical I " in faith " is—unity in community, in the historical community which I believe to be the communion of Christ. Because the humanity wherein I stand, which I myself also am, prays for me, forgives sins (in preaching and sacrament) independently of me, being always the whole humanity whereever I am, just because I am its member, my everydayness is overcome within the communion: only there am I embraced both as individual and as humanity, in existentiality and continuity—but of course only " in faith ", which knows itself possible by virtue of the communion and is abolished within it.

The indestructible unity of my I is guaranteed even while it crumbles into everydayness: ὅ δὲ νῦν ζῶ ἐν σαρκί, ἐν πίστει ζῶ (Gal. 2, 20).

Faith is " with reference to " being—the Christian communion—conversely, it is only in faith that this being reveals itself or " is ", yet faith knows it to be independent of itself, and knows itself to be a manner of being *of* that being. Being transcends entity: it is the basis of the entity and the I alike. Thus act comes from being, as it also goes to being. Being, moreover, has reference to act, yet is free. The being of revelation, as hovering between the objective and the non-objective, is " person "—the revealed person of God and the personal community of which that person is the foundation. Here the transcendental thesis of " being only in the act ", and the original ontological principle of being independent of the act, unexpectedly coalesce. Of course, if being is understood as entity, with a phenomeno-logical system of autonomous self-understanding as corollary, the result is as incompatible with the idea of revelation as is Kant's rational transcendentalism.

Since the transcendental and ontological theses are here combined in the sociological category, the existence of man is conceived to lie as essentially in decision as in " already being in Christ (or Adam) ". For though faith is act, yet, as the manner of being in the Church of Christ, it embraces the whole of existence in Christ, just as unbelief, as the manner of being in Adam, embraces the whole of the old existence. Faith knows that it comes to its decision as to one already decided. Just as unbelief is no discrete psychic act but is the manner of being in the old humanity, so belief[1] may correctly be seen not only as an act but as the manner of being in the Church of Christ. One may therefore " stand in faith " (I Cor. 16, 13; II Cor. 1, 24; Eph. 6, 14; I Thess. 3, 8; I Peter 5, 12) as in the " decided decision " without a conscious act of faith; but this is not a general principle, for faith alone may assert it.

As the being of God does not have the mode of " there is ", so this applies also to the being of human existence whether

---

[1] Cf. p. 100, n.1, above. (*Translator.*)

133

in sin or in faith. " There is " no believer, no sinner;
" there is " no " given " human existence, *qua* encountered,
but it " is ", by virtue of the Word of God, in the execution
of acts within the Church—in which same acts the unity of
the existence is affirmed. Here again the " thing "-con-
ception of being is set in motion by the category of social
reference.

If in faith the whole man is to be embraced by the communion of Christ, sin and death must be contained, yet
their " intention " is to disrupt the continuity of the new
being. Sin and death, therefore, reach into the communion
of Christ, but this they do in such a way that the communion now bears with me my sin and my death, while
I likewise no longer see sin and death in the communion—in
Christ himself [1]—but only forgiveness and life. My sin is
no longer a sin, my death is no longer a death, because the
communion is with me. It is temptation which will have
me believe that sin can finally put me beyond the pale of
God's commonwealth, or that death is my eternal con-
demnation: the temptation of the $\sigma\acute{\alpha}\rho\xi$ which endures
while I live $\grave{\epsilon}\nu$ $\sigma\alpha\rho\kappa\acute{\iota}$. Here is the application of *pecca
fortiter, sed fortius fide et gaude in Christo.*[2] And so through
the communion, because it bears the entire historical
man, faith can embrace the whole of historical life in
everydayness, sin and death, for the new being whose manner
it is must impinge on existence and be in continuity.

[1] Cf. Luther's Sermon on the Holy Body of Jesus, W. A., 2, 742ff.,
especially 746ff., and Tesseradecas, W. A., 6, 130ff.

[2] Luther, Enders, III, 208, 119.

D. *The problem of knowledge and the idea of the Church*

We have yet to discuss the concept of knowledge which corresponds to the being of revelation and the being of man.

1. The endeavour to regard revelation as non-objective and make it thus indirectly the object of cognition means that when I speak of revelation I always take into account whatever God may have to say further to or against it; it means that I always counter a judgment of knowing with another of not-knowing, that the obligation of God to his Word is limited by the freedom of God which is beyond all binding; in other words, I include in my thinking a factor which renders it a priori uncertain, a factor which consists in my adding the antithesis to the positive proposition. That is Barth's dialectic.[1]

Man's knowing is not-knowing.[2] Only on this understanding is it possible for God to have free speech, to remain at all times a subject [3] (supposing that God *is* only in the God-effected existential act of faith, never in reflexion). We see here the interconnection of the actwise interpreta-

---

[1] That at least is its general sense. To speak frankly, I do not think it is possible, when one looks more closely, to lay hold of any unequivocal concept of dialectic in Barth. Thus when I collate *Dogmatik*, I, p. 456, Section *b*, lines 1–3 and 9, with p. 457, lines 5ff., and p. 460, lines 6ff., I think to detect a confusion of three entirely different concepts of theological dialectic, which do not all describe, even, the same aim and concern: one might rather say they leave doubt as to whether dialectic is here a method separable from the heart of the matter (cf. Schumann, op. cit., pp. 221ff.) or whether Barth's whole case does not in fact stand or fall with it.

[2] Cf. *Dogmatik*, I, p. 61.

[3] Idem, p. 64.

tion, dialectic and the non-objective concept of knowledge. To this may be objected: (*a*) The whole conceptual nexus is conceived individualistically. If revelation has an essential reference to the community, God must in some way be bound quite apart from my individual act. (*b*) His being bound to the Church is the freedom of God. To leave open any freedom of God beyond the event of salvation is to formalize, to *rationalise*, the contingent positivity of that event. (*c*) we "know" from preaching of the revelation given to the Church. Theologically this knowing takes three forms: disbelieving, existential and ecclesiastical; what these mean will be made clear later. It is wrong to say that there is generally speaking a not-knowing, inferred from an idealistic-rationalistic anthropology, which corresponds to the "knowing" of revelation; once we believe, if it *is* belief in faith, we know without not-knowing. There must be, that is, a knowing which stands in faith, i.e. in the communion. We can know what is given to us (I Cor. 2, 12). How knowing then becomes positive knowledge (*Wissen, Wissenschaft*) is another question and a later stage. (*d*) It is a fateful error on Barth's part to replace the Lord and creator with the concept of the subject. In the first place, it means that I have God always at my back, with the result that I must be content with dialectical theology's permanent reflexion on its own faith instead of having direct recourse to Christ; the seal is set on God's non-objectivity. A further consequence is that God is virtually defined as the subject of my new existence, of my theological thinking, instead of as Lord and creator of both. Here the transcendental view of the act, prospectively and retrospectively oriented "with reference to" the transcendental, is as well served—in fact better served—by the idea of the Lord and creator as by the concept of the subject. But the ultimate reason for the inadequacy of Barth's explanation lies in the fact that it fails to understand God as a person. From this failure arises a defective definition of the being of revelation, whence a defective concept of knowledge. When we come to ask what truth remains in the interpretation of the act which underlies the non-objective concept of knowledge, we must extract our answer from the result of defining the being of revelation as personal, accepting whatever consequences may follow for the concept of knowledge itself.

2. To the being of revelation, defined as that of the Christ-person in the community of persons called the Church, defined therefore in sociological terms, there must correspond a concept of knowledge envisaged in a sociological category. In understanding this we first need to distinguish between three ways of knowing, hence three concepts, which correspond to distinct sociological functions of the Church: knowing as a *believer*, knowing in *preaching* and *theological* knowledge, of which the first may be called *existential* and the others *ecclesiastical* cognition:

Knowing as a *believer* is a question of fundamental sociological epistemology. It means knowing oneself overcome and blessed with grace by the person of Christ through the preached Word. Whether such cognition is possible is a senseless question here,[1] since it derives, as framed, from the isolation of unbelief, whence it can only be answered

[1] See for example Barth, op. cit., § 6, 2: " Die Möglichkeit des Hörens "; § 17: " Die subjektive Möglichkeit der Offenbarung".

Act and Being

with an Impossible! (*incapax!*). The asking of such a question postulates a concept of existence as potentiality. But faith is a God-given *reality:* one may question its manner of being or becoming, its How, but not the actual fact of its being. Its object is the person of Christ which is preached within the communion. This is an object which resists inclusion in a transcendental I, or any non-objectification: it stands as person over against man as person. The person is a unity which overrides the bifurcation of " entity " and non-entity; it is objective, i.e. knowable, yet by virtue of its genuine *ob*-jectivity, its freedom from the knower, freedom *not* to be (*Nichtseinkönnen*),[1] it never falls into the power of the knowing I. It gives itself through the Word to the I in the act of faith, which for its part acknowledges the freedom of the self-giving person and testifies thus to its absolute extrinsicality. If however the person in revelation should withdraw from cognition, there remains only the " Word " as held in remembrance, to which only the person itself can restore its power over human existence of freedom-not-to-be —the power of acknowledged extrinsicality. If the I as

[1] By *Nichtseinkönnen* Bonhoeffer presumably designates the person's freedom not to be an entity or cognitive object, its ability to withhold itself from a cognitive intention. On the knowability of persons there are interesting pages in Max Scheler's *Vom Ewigen im Menschen*, in " Probleme der Religion ", Section 2. The knowing of persons is of course in itself a distinctive kind of knowing: for " knowable ", in the annotated sentence, Bonhoeffer uses both *erkennbar* and *wissbar*; briefly, they are distinguished in his usage by the employment of *erkennen* to designate the instantaneous acquisition of knowledge, the typical " epistemological " act, and of *wissen* for knowing as positive storable knowledge, knowledge one can " live in ", whence *Wissenschaft*—a compendium of such. The importance of *Wissen* here is that it implies continuity; to postulate its possibility with respect to God is to uphold (*contra* Barth) the respectability of a positive theology. (*Translator.*)

person suffers the impact of the person of Christ in judgment or in the process of incorporation into the communion, it cannot conceive that this having-to-suffer derives from itself but must recognise that it comes from outside. Herein lies the peculiarity of the theo-sociological category.

In the communion, the extrinsicality sought in individualistic epistemology is a given reality, one which, as a contingent pre-requisite, can no longer be called into question, nor stabilised by a " there is " and turned into something " there for the finding " of cognition. The extrinsicality of the Christ-person is essentially transcendent of existence, yet it " is " only in its action on human existence. It is not that of the external world, but the peculiar extrinsicality of the Christ-person claiming my whole personal existence both as guilty and as forgiven: the extrinsicality of the theo-sociological category, which is only known for truly *extrinsic* where man is *in* Christ.

But through the person of Christ the I's fellow-man is also rescued from the world of things, to which he of course continues to belong *qua* entity, and drawn into the social sphere of persons. Only through Christ does my neighbour confront me as making some form of absolute claim on me from a position outside my own existence. Only here is reality sheer first-hand decision. Without Christ my very neighbour is no more than my possibility of self-assertion through " sustaining his claim " (Grisebach).

And so it is that through the extrinsicality of the Christ-person the *external world* takes on fresh meaning. But even the external world, as mediator of the spirit of Christ, (here including the empirical Church) should not be classified in the sphere of " there is ". " There is " presupposes the position of the *detached* observer, which with regard to the being of revelation is inapplicable even to the external world, i.e. creation, since the being of revelation is the very basis of my being a person. The judgment, therefore, that " there is " this person is a reflexion, which has already fallen away from direct reference and bears merely upon the residual entity. One must digest and be constantly mindful of this, that the personal mode of being *is being* no less than the mode of " there is ", and—though the point may be left open for the present—that the first mode is almost certainly the foundation of the second.

Thus faith discloses a new sphere of knowledge and objects, that of existence in the social reference, which replaces other concepts of knowledge. The sociological category has served to redefine the " outside ", the " boundary " (cf. p. 31 above). Dilthey's attempt was perhaps the first to reduce the problem of transcendence to the historical (*geschichtlich*) problem of the encounter of two personal wills (see p. 43, n. 1, above). Yet even this attempt has no issue or fulfilment save in revelation's encounter of the divine person and man.

Now we have found that in our sociological category we have the point of union of the transcendental and the onto-logical epistemologies. The person " is " only in the self-giving act. And yet the person " is " in independence of that to which it gives itself. It is through the person of Christ that we acquire this understanding of the person, which applies only to the Christ-based personal community of the Christian Church. The Christ preached in the communion gives himself to the member of the communion.

Faith means knowing that one has reference to this. In faith I " have " Christ in his personal objectivity, i.e. as my Lord who has power over me, atones for me, redeems me. In faith there is no not-knowing, for there Christ is his own witness and confirmation.

In faith Christ is the creator of my new personal being and at the same time the Lord " with reference to " which —εἰς αὐτόν—the person is created; thus existence is determined both prospectively and retrospectively in relation to transcendence: it " is " between transcendent poles. In the act of belief, which Christ himself creates within me, inasmuch as he gives me the Holy Spirit who hears and believes within me, he also proves himself the free Lord of my existence. Christ " is " only " in " faith, yet he is master of my faith. He is the absolute extrinsicality for my existence, but for that very reason he impinges on it, gives himself to be known by it.

As concrete being-assailed by Christ, the movement of faith passes in time, though not ascertainably in demonstrable theres and thens. Where and when I believed is known only to God and is inaccessible to my reflexion. Faith abides in itself as *actus directus* (see pp. 102f. above, also Part Three below). Nothing could be more mistaken than to deny, from the fact that everything is accessible to reflexion only *in* reflexion—therefore faith only as " faith-wishful-ness " (" *Gläubigkeit* "), " religiosity "—that there is an *actus directus* taking place in time. For such a dismissal reflexion has no justification. Reflexion discovers itself always to be already in reflexion, and this very reflexion must indicate that connection to the direct act has been interrupted. This is the fundamental problem of everyday-

ness. Although by its very nature my faith, as a temporal
act, embraces the whole of my existence and though it (or
my existence) is abolished in being within the communion
(see p. 130 above),[1] for *reflexion* there remains only the past
spoken Word of Christ as a general proposition, as " meaning " in " remembrance ". The person and the Word have
separated, and we are left with the condition of predicatory
and theological knowledge.

The *preacher*, as one who addresses the communion, must
" know " what he preaches: Jesus Christ the crucified
(I Cor. 2, 2). He has full power to announce the gospel to
the hearer, to forgive sins in preaching and sacrament.
There may be no uncertainty here, no not-knowing: all
must be made plain from the Word of God who has bound
himself in revelation, for in the preaching which produces
faith Christ causes himself to be declared the " subject " of
the spoken words. I preach, that is, but I preach in the
strength of Christ, the strength of my faith, for, given that
during the preaching itself I could overcome temptation in
the act of faith, the existential proposition that " I have
been forgiven " would in itself be no vehicle of the ecclesiastical " thou art forgiven ", which depends on the community whose office preaching is. For that reason preaching
is in principle always heard.

Notwithstanding, the preacher himself must reflect on
the matter of his address, the Word of the Crucified, and
must bring it to expression. Thus through the manner of
his utterance, which involves reflexion, its matter also
becomes problematic. For over against reflexion stand

[1] Of course this too is only a statement from faith.

only general " propositions ", " words " in " remembrance " about a divine event. These the preacher can reiterate, but he is unable to speak the living, creative Word of the Christ-person itself.

Now to preaching, as office of the communion, is given the promise that when the preacher correctly utters the " words " and " propositions " (pure doctrine—*recte docetur*) the living person of Christ attests itself therein, inasmuch as it discloses itself to the hearer. But how is it possible for the preacher to speak " correctly " if he can only " propose "?

This sets the problem of *theological* cognition, hence the question: how is theological science possible?

Theology is a function of the Church, for Church there is none without preaching, nor preaching without remembrance, but theology is the memory of the Church. As such it assists the Church to understand the premises of Christian preaching; helps it, in other words, to form dogmas. To this end it must have positive knowledge (*Wissen*) of the Christian affair; how is such knowledge possible?

In theological reflexion I am detached from the intentionality of the faith which vanquishes temptation. So theological is not existential knowledge. It has its object in the remembered happenings of the Christian communion, the Bible, preaching and sacrament, prayer, confession, the Word of the Christ-person which is stored as entity in the historical Church. Theology is therefore the science which has its own premises as its object, which is as much as to say that it stands between past and future preaching. Theology should link past preaching to the real person of Christ, as he preaches and is preached in the communion, and in this way there should be proposed to future preaching a dogma on the basis of which it can preach with Christian rectitude. It follows that logically dogma is not the aim but the condition of preaching.

It seems, then that in principle theological is not different from profane thought. Dogmatic knowledge is positive knowledge reflecting on entity, therefore is in principle amenable to grouping within a system. Even the connection with the living person of Christ is reflective and as such systematic. Yet if the connection is genuine it has been made possible not by the pursuit of any theoretic method but by cleaving to the heard Word in humility; here, despite the foregoing, theological differs in essence from all profane science, not in method of thinking but in obedience of thought. In itself the dialectical method of the reservation is no humbler than an avowedly systematic thought. Moreover, dialectical thought, as such, has no immediate claim to existential force. On the contrary, humility in theology is impossible so long as it gives out its propositions as existential or as faith-inspired (which in the end is the same thing); theological thought and knowledge are only possible as *ecclesiastical* thought and knowledge. Because theology turns revelation into entity, it may only be practised where the living person of Christ is itself present to acknowledge or destroy that entity. On that account theology must stand in intimate relationship with preaching, preparing its way, yet on the other hand submitting humbly to its direction. It is positive science, for it has its own given object, the *spoken* Word of Christ in the Church, from which fact it has authority to make general pronouncements; it aims at the system, at dogma. But it is only within the Christian communion that all this acquires its particular meaning. Only the communion knows that the Word it hears is ever and again repeated in a sphere beyond theology, that theology is no more than the custodian, catalogue and memorial of this Word; it knows that the general pronouncements are meaningless without their confirmation by Christ, knows that the very dogma on which preaching builds is the result of " direction " by preaching. It knows that when theology says " God forgives sins " neither God himself nor sin itself is implicated, but that both have been used to form a general proposition, for there is real talk of God and sin only when Christ speaks of them here and now, speaks of my sin specifically in the existential " now ". In sum, theology is unable to speak creatively, but once the community of Christ is aware of its theology's limitations it may and should take courage to practise it. Then it may " know " even as Paul " knew " (Rom. 6, 9; I Cor. 2, 2; 2, 12; II Cor. 4, 14; 5, 1; Eph. 1, 9), in the manner not of existential, not of speculative, but of *ecclesiastical knowledge*. It may be certain of the faithfulness of God, who stands by the Word he has given to his community, so that theology, if it but earnestly place itself within the communion, can never go wholly astray. For the communion needs theology.

Needless to say, theology can never conquer the real temptations of faith with its propositions. It is a matter of the concrete struggle, taking place in the direct consciousness of man, between Christ and Satan, of which the issue must first be won and lost. We may keep before our eyes, as much as we like, theological propositions of forgiveness and redemption; unless Christ in person speaks to us his Word of new creation to transform our existence, unless the general proposition becomes a living occurrence, they themselves are a collective temptation.

Here are the bounds of theology. This is known by the communion in which it is practised, and indeed it would appear only in the knowledge of its limitations, but also of its justice and necessity, that theology's tendency to " self-justification by intellectual works " (Herrmann) can be overcome. In the final analysis, it is only because dialectical theology thinks individualistically, i.e. in constant abstractions, that it takes its own method more seriously than is consonant with its own premises. In reality the position is such that I, speaking as theologian, can counter the urge to justify myself with intellectual works in no other way than by inserting my theology into the communion of persons (which is the theologian's humility), and allowing the communion to allocate its place, bestow its meaning upon it. Thought, even theological thought, will always be " systematic " by nature and can therefore never comprehend the living person of Christ, yet there is obedient and there is disobedient thinking (II Cor. 10, 5): it is obedient when it does not abstract itself from the Church which alone can shake and rouse it from the systematic, the Church in which alone it has meaning.

For preaching it follows that the preacher must be a theologian. But predicatory differs from theological cognition in the special circumstances whereby the preacher has to utter the Word before an empirical assembly of the historical communion. Thus the object of this cognition is no longer the already spoken Word but the Word to be spoken here and now to this assembly. This Word is not spoken as an existential confession, nor as pure theological doctrine from the very pulpit; everything hinges on the office. The preacher, knowing that at this very moment, in this very place, through his very self, Christ wishes to address the communion, announces the gospel in the full power of the communion, and for the hearer this Word is a word of decision. For himself as a separate individual the preacher may not cease to pray " help Thou my unbelief ", but for himself as ordained to the office of preacher to the congregation he utters that prayer no more. As that of an individual the preacher's cognition is also reflexive, second-hand; as borne by the office it is productive, not reproductive, and plenipotentiary. The only possible vehicle of the proposition " thou art forgiven " is the office, but that is namely Christ and his communion themselves; the individual is permitted to declare that forgiveness because he must, because the communion wishes to hear it.

Sociologically, the preacher is primarily, essentially, in the communion and secondarily an individual, whereas the dogmatist is essentially an individual and secondarily in the communion. The believer, however, is in essence equally an individual and a member of the communion.

To resume: in the knowing of the believer there is absolutely no reflexion. The question whether faith is possible can be answered only by faith's reality. But, since this reality retires from demonstration as an entity, any reflexion must obliterate it. Faith looks not on itself, but on

Christ alone. Whether faith *is* faith can be neither ascertained nor even believed, but the faith which believes *is* faith.

That such faith takes place in the " direct consciousness " is as certain as that it is not reflexively reproducible in its actwise reality, wherefore one may never say: on this or that occasion, at such and such a place, I believed.

If the object of the believer's knowing is the living Word of Christ, that of theological cognition is the spoken Word, that of predicatory cognition the Word to be spoken and declared to the communion. As the action of an individual, predicatory is no less reflexive than theological cognition, but in the office of the congregation to whom he must declare the forgiveness of sins the preacher sees his knowledge as that of the communion, therefore as appointed with authority to edify the communion.

Let us return to the mainstream of our inquiry. The general investigation must conclude, we now see, with the problem of a theological doctrine of man's self-understanding in connection with his " being placed into truth " by revelation. " In faith " man understands himself to be within the Church in his new being: he knows this as an existential reality which lay outside the bounds of his own peculiar potentialities. He sees his existence founded solely by the Word of the person of Christ. He lives *sub specie Dei* and otherwise not at all. Being is to be in Christ; here alone is unity and wholeness of life; and so he comes to know that his old being was being in Adam. The being of man has no formal, metaphysical, psychological properties dissociable from the proposition that " man is either in Christ or in Adam " (see Part Three).

Act and Being

Man is connected with truth, " refers to " truth, because he " is " in truth. This truth is no longer the self-imposed extreme of the self-transparent I (though, even in the case of that " truth ", one's connection consisted in one's being in it). This truth is one bestowed, revealed; it is Jesus Christ himself; the connection of existence to him is a positive connection [1] (*justitia passiva!*). But because here untruth is placed into truth, unlike is known by unlike (cf. pp. 41f. above). Thus the mediator must always be the "sense ", the " lucid " Word, though not as if from this, as from a " given " meaning of man, were to grow the possibility of autonomous self-understanding. But through this medium of meaning, unlike gives itself to be known by unlike—Christ the crucified and risen by man, who himself lives. While God knows [2] man, man knows God. But to be known by God means to become a new man. Thus it is at once the sinner and the just man who know God. It is not because God's Word makes " sense " that it affects the existence of man but because it is the Word of *God*—

[1] *. . . ist eine gesetzte Beziehung.* Here, presumably, *gesetzt* also means " imposed from without ", as opposed to the " self-imposed " (*selbst-gesetzt*) of idealism. But it does not therefore mean " scientifically objective "; though God institutes, ordains, makes positive the connection, it is not necessarily " pre-"ordained in the man of nature (fallen Adam)—cf. preceding paragraph. Man is not man (as pure creature), lacks his essentials, until he is existentially in Christ. The *jus* of *justitia* is synonymous with the *Gesetz* of *gesetzt*: the true law or normal order for man (Bonhoeffer seems to imply) is the existential, i.e. *extra*-ordinary, in which his " being " is Christ. (*Translator.*)

[2] " Know ", here, is the usual " epistemological " word—*erkennen*. But in this context the act-connotation of intention must be stressed in order to distinguish the sense from that of " A knows B " when this means " A is acquainted with B ". Here *erkennen* is existential; the everyday sense demands " A *kennt* B ". (*Translator.*)

of the Creator, Atoner, Redeemer; yet it is in "sense" that this Word is fulfilled, even if that meaning is counter-sense, non-sense. Thus man, when he understands himself in faith, is wholly ravished from his own sense and redirected to God.

For theology, however, this self-understanding in the instant of belief, under the onslaught of Christ on my existence, can only be stored in a recollection. It is this understanding which is removed by two stages of reflexion when I under-stand myself to this extent: that I "can" only understand-myself-in-recollection. For such is the theologian's reflexion on himself. He knows that his doctrine of human self-understanding is limited, by his own self-understanding and circumstances, to "only ever being able to understand oneself in recollection"; he could not overreach himself, unless Christ were to tempt and overcome him, in which case he would no longer be the theologian. And so his anthropology remains a theory like any other; likewise the concrete doctrine of self-understanding in revelation which is unfolded in these pages is, in itself, mere theory, system, autonomous self-understanding. Only in the Church itself, where the Word of Christ is held in remembrance and his living person is active, is it understood that a theology meaning to serve the concrete Church is in reality sub-serving, as autonomous thought, the nomos of Christ. Where a theological self-understanding is concerned, it is no longer a case of "self-understanding which has been placed into truth"—*that* it is in faith—but of "reflexive thought in the service of the Church". If one may adapt

Luther's dictum, the theologian's rubric is *Reflecte fortiter, sed fortius fide et gaude in Christo.*

Nothing of this tends to justify any particular theology. On the contrary, we discover the enterprise of theology to be based on the structure of the Church and to be justifiable only in that context. Which particular theology is right is something for dogma to say, but dogma is " directed " by the preaching of the living Christ.

PART THREE

The Act-Being Problem in the Concrete Doctrine of Man "In Adam" or "in Christ"

BEING IN ADAM

A. *Definition of " being " in Adam*

Sola fide credendum est nos esse peccatores.[1] " To be in Adam " is a more pointed ontological equivalent of *esse peccator*. It derives from the Bible (I Cor. 15, 22; cf. 15, 45; Rom. 5, 12–14). If it were humanly possible to know oneself a sinner without revelation, neither " being in Adam " nor " being in Christ " would be an existential definition of man's being, for it would mean that man could place himself into truth and could therefore turn back from his being *qua* sinner (i.e. his not being in truth) to some more fundamental being of his own, hence being in Adam would have to be regarded as the potentiality of a deeper " ability to be in truth ", as resting on a being untouched by sin. Theologically expressed, this would mean that the sinner remains the creature, existence as a creature providing the substratum of the ontic modulation which is sinnerhood. If in this way it is contested that the whole of man's being is involved in his being a sinner, there is danger of semi-Pelagianism; ontologically, the doctrine of *causae secundae* becomes unavoidable. Seen in this light, Luther's words

[1] Luther, *Röm. Komm.*, Ficker, II, pp. 69, 12ff.

are thus intelligible: we may never comprehend our existence as a whole, because it is founded solely on God's Word: God's Word demands faith. That we are sinners in the whole of our being is a knowledge accessible only to faith in revelation, for it is only then, by God's Word, that the whole of our being can be placed into truth.

That is revealed knowledge which outside revelation (i.e. in Adam) can never be acquired, for " in Adam " means in untruth, in culpable perversion of the will (the human essence) inwards to the self—*cor curvum in se*. Man has broken loose from communion with God, thus also with men, and now he stands alone, which is in untruth.[1] Because he is alone, the world is " his " world, his fellow-men have sunk into the world of things (cf. Heidegger's " *Mitsein* "), God has become a religious object, but man himself has become his own creator, his own master and property. That he should now begin and end with himself in his cognition is only to be expected, for he is utterly " by himself " in the falsehood of naked self-lordship.

Ontologically this means that sin is the violation of the

[1] H. F. Kohlbrügge, *Das siebente Kapitel des Briefes Pauli an die Römer*, 1839, p. 52: Man " did not lose the image of God but lost God himself, and after he had become disobedient God called him ' flesh ' and his conduct ' wicked ', ' sin '. How has man been behaving since? He makes use of the properties wherein he has been created by God just as if he had not become a transgressor through the disobedience of *one*, as if he had not fallen, as if his entire heart, devisings, notions, deliberations, as if himself as he is and lives, were not perverted and perverse. . . . He makes use of *life* in order to deny his *death*, or *righteousness* to set up his own self-righteousness, whereupon to insist that he disclaims his own righteousness. . . . He makes use of *truth* to make God a liar, to tear himself loose from God where he is bound to him, and to bind God to him with a Word which—as he reads it—has not come to him ".

Dasein (the being of the creature) by the *Wie-Sein*,[1] that when we come to the concept of sin this ontological distinction between *Da-* and *Wie-Sein* is meaningless, because the I has become its own master and itself taken possession of its existence. Furthermore, the knowledge of sinnerhood is impossible from the state of sin itself, because the *Dasein* is still in the power of the *Wiesein*; it can be derived only from revelation, wherein creatureliness and sin are separated in a manner which remains to be described. And so the ontological definition of man as being a sinner, as existing in sin " with reference to " God, remains correct. Any attempt to establish an ontological principle by fastening the idea of the creature to " Adam " must lead to the Catholicism of the *analogia entis*, a pure metaphysics of being. The thought and philosophy of man in sin is self-glorifying, even when it purports to question itself as " critical philosophy ", so long as it will not allow revelation to drive it into the historical Church of Christ; all knowledge, not excluding γνῶθι σεαυτόν, is bent on man's ultimate justification in his own eyes. But there comes a time when, under the Atlas-burden of a world's creator, in the cold silence of his eternal solitude, man begins to fear himself, to shudder in alarm. Thereupon, exalting himself to be his own final judge, he proceeds to his own indictment—which is couched in the language of conscience. His answer, when charged, is remorse (*contritio activa!*). The conscience and remorse of man in Adam are his final

[1] *Dasein* and *Wiesein*, " thereness " and " howness ", mean respectively the actual being (existence) and manner or quality of being (what we have rendered above as " ontic modulation "). In the rest of Part Three these German words will be retained when used in contrast. (*Translator.*)

157

grasp at himself, the final confirmation and justification of his self-lordly, self-masterly attitude.[1] Man makes himself the defendant and exhorts himself upward to his better self. But the cry of conscience serves only to dissemble the mute loneliness of his desolate isolation, it sounds without echo into the world that is governed and construed by the self. Man in Adam reaches the confines of his solitude but, mis-reading his situation, continues to " seek himself in himself "[2]; he hopes by remorse still to preserve his sinful existence.[3] As a sinner he abides by his sins, for he sees them through his conscience, which holds him prisoner in himself and bids him look only on those sins, but " sin grows also and waxes great through too much looking and thinking on it; to which contributes the foolishness of our conscience, that is ashamed before God and sorely punishes itself ".[4] There-fore this conscience is of the Devil,[5] who leaves man to himself in untruth, so this conscience must be mortified when Christ comes to man. Conscience can torture, can drive to despair, but is unable of itself to kill man, because indeed it is his final grasp at himself.[6] Man is unable to

[1] But against this see for example Brunstäd, op. cit., p. 226: ". . . the value-reality of the unconditional-personal is evidenced in the con-science ".

[2] Luther, W.A. 2, 690.

[3] Luther, W.A. 2, 719: " in which belief, if it were possible that thou hadst the remorse of all the world, yet it would be the remorse of Judas, which rather angers than placates God ".

[4] Luther, W.A. 2, 687, 689: " Therefore thou shouldst not look on the sin in the sinners nor in thy conscience. . . ."

[5] Luther, W.A. 40, 511. On the *duo diaboli,* cf. W.A. 40, 1. 74.

[6] This was put with admirable clarity by H. F. Kohlbrügge, op. cit., pp. 27f.: " For sin does not only lurk behind evil; even more it lurks behind good. . . . If we now do good, sin permits us to renounce evil before God, helps us to pray and weep, strive and struggle, till we faint

will his own death even in conscience.[1] There is his limit;
he clings to himself, therefore his knowledge of himself is
imprisoned in untruth.[2] To be placed in truth in the sight
of God means to be dead or to live, but these are conditions
neither of which man can impose on himself, they are
conferred on him only by the encounter with Christ in
contritio passiva and faith. It is only when Christ has broken
through the solitude of man that man knows himself placed
into truth; whether, in the challenge with which the Cross
confronts the sinner, man dies for ever, persisting in his

---

and sink; thus does it drive and goad us to maintain through this very
care our wretchedness in the sight of God. . . . For such piety and
holiness is well-pleasing to the flesh. Here is penance, absolution and
a constant unmindfulness of the purification of bygone sins, yet man
himself stays fast in the death which is the flesh, and only to maintain
himself in the same he wills the good . . ., that he may procure himself
rest in his unrest. . . ." And on p. 29: " I made a thousand protests
against all wicked desires, I sundered myself from my flesh, armed
myself with tears, exercises of penance and tireless prayer; I cried out
for the spirit of God that it might sanctify me through and through,
I believed, I did works: but all that I did as one pressed by necessity,
not from love of God's commandments; I shunned the will of God
even while I strove to act in accord with it. . . . Nay, I did good out
of enmity to God. . . ." And on p. 37: " Then it plagued me with
sins and let me soon after feel remorse, that I might not come to be
aware that I fell short of God's glory. . . ." And on p. 40: " This is
the sin of us all, this the high-priest in the temple of the religiosity of all
flesh, who, applying to his service the service of God, kills all that is
under the sun".

[1] Luther, W.A. 18, 664.
[2] Luther, W.A. 18, 674: " *Caeca est enim natura humana, ut nesciat suas
ipsius vires seu morbos potius, deinde superba videtur sibi nosse et posse omnia . . .
scriptura autem definit hominem esse corruptum et captum, tum superbe contem-
nentem et ignorantem suae corruptionis et captivitatis.*

isolation, or dies to live in truth with Christ (for die he must, as Christ died), in either case true knowledge of oneself is given only through Christ. If " thought knowing itself master of its world " corresponded to the condition of isolation, this state is now recognised in its true colours as guilt towards Christ; that is to say, it is only recognised for what it is at the instant of Christ's break-through. If conscience made a direct line of communication between man and God, it would circumvent God's self-obligation to the mediating Word, hence exclude Christ and the Church.[1]

Moreover, the temptation which leads to man's death is itself the work of Christ, for man dies of the law only because Christ died or (in the pre-Christian era) was to die through the law. The severest temptation of the law, of the *deus in sua majestate*,[2] is temptation by the death of Christ as end.[3] It is in principle not possible to lay down the difference between real temptation by Christ and temptation by conscience, as the last grasp of the self at the self; this difference is analogous to the relation of faith and faith-wishfulness. Where the I has truly come to the end, truly reaches out of itself, where its grasp is more than a final " seeking of the self in the self ", there Christ is at work. However, certainty about this is never to be won by reflexion on the act—we remain psychologically self-impenetrable—

---

[1] It is probably no idle coincidence that Holl both defines Luther's religion as one of conscience and admits a possibility of finding, in the first commandment, God without Christ. Cf. *Luther*,[3] p. 70.

[2] In Luther, the essential implication of this expression is that of a God not bound by the Word of grace. It is not, however, intended to imply an impossibility of meeting the *deus in sua majestate* in Christ.

[3] Literal translation. (*Translator.*)

but only in the direct contemplation of Christ and his activity upon me, within me. Hence Luther's countless admonitions not to look on one's own remorse, own faith, but to look on the Lord Christ himself. While I am still reflecting on myself in order to find Christ, Christ is not there. If he is really there, I see only him. Conscience may be termed the voice of God only inasmuch as conscience is where, in the real temptation, Christ kills man—in order to give or not give him life.[1] It is all-important to know that self-understanding is possible only when and where the living Christ approaches us, only in his comtemplation. αὐτοὶ ἐν ἑαυτοῖς ἑαυτοὺς μετροῦντες καὶ συγκρίνοντες ἑαυτοὺς οὐ τυνιᾶσιν (II Cor. 10, 12).

But, because the attempt to understand oneself from oneself remains in sin, as formal ontology the definition of

[1] With reference to the current debate on conscience cf. Holl's *Luther*, Brunstäd's *Idee der Religion* and the work by Hirsch, *Jesus Christus, der Herr*. All three credit Luther with a " religion of conscience ". On the other side are to be placed Gogarten's criticism of Holl in *Christliche Welt*, 1924, his *Ich glaube an den dreieinigen Gott*, 1926, his *Theologische Tradition und theologische Arbeit*, 1927, and Grisebach's *Gegenwart*, 1928. In the last, see for example pp. 564ff.: " And so restraints are imposed upon me through the experience of conscience, from myself and never but through myself, but in this way the restraints are never really imposed from without. That is just the astounding thing about conscience: man hears only himself in an ultimate and frightful isolation, and he therefore thinks to be hearing himself as God. . . ." And on p. 475: " It would be overrating oneself to maintain that in one's essential nature one could hear the voice of the actual basis of ethical reality". H. M. Müller evinces a large measure of agreement with Grisebach in his *Erfahrung und Glaube bei Luther*, 1929. See further pp. 267–300 of Heidegger's *Sein und Zeit*, 1927, G. Jacob's *Der Gewissensbegriff in der Theologie Luthers*, 1930, which is influenced by Heidegger and Tillich, and R. Seeberg's article " Gewissen " in *R.G.G.*, II. Stoker's *Das Gewissen*, 1925, is relevant to the phenomenology of conscience.

human existence in Adam as sinnerhood is correct and sufficient. To being in sin corresponds the act of self-misunderstanding through the usurpation of the *Dasein* by the *Wiesein*,[1] in the sinful act of pretending to absolute power over oneself. The interrelation of act and being " in Adam " is something we now have to examine.

B. " *Adam* " *as I and as humanity*

Sin is the narcissism of the human will, which is to say " essence ". Will has no reality save as free and conscious, therefore sin must be understood as act. Any choice made in a self-seeking sense must be adjudged a sinful act. The importance of defining sin in this way lies in this, that it does not seem otherwise possible to preserve the guilt-character of sin; underlying this as an empirical datum is the dictate of conscience, to the effect that one is responsible only for *wilful* self-determination against God. Here one may attempt to differentiate sin and guilt as respectively being and act, but in the (empirical) light of one's conscience it seems false to understand sin-*qua*-guilt as the being of man, and so to minimise the gravity of guilt as a distinct concept. Sin, then, is act. Fundamental to this conclusion is a concept of conscience as God's direct voice in man. But if we accept a different explanation of the experience of conscience, such as was outlined above, this argument fails. The endeavour of conscience to restrict sin to the act should be regarded as man's attempt at self-salvation. We have knowledge of what sin is only through Christ's mediation of God's Word, and this knowledge overrules whatever con-

[1] See p. 157, n. 1, above (*Translator*).

science may have to say in dissent. *Sola fide credendum est nos esse peccatores.*

If sin were no more than the occasional free act, it would be theoretically and humanly possible to find one's way back to a sinless being; revelation in Christ would have become redundant. The death of Christ reveals that the whole man must die to the law, since the whole of the old Adam is in sin. The continuity of man's being in Adam is judged by the death of Christ. Thus the necessity arises of understanding sin as being.

There are two ways in which sin may be understood as having the " entity " mode of being:

1. By embodiment in the doctrine of original sin: we may call the process historicisation, psychologisation or naturalisation. In one way or another sin is fastened to the nature of man as humanly generated. In this tarnished nature, *non possum non peccare.* The concept of nature vouches a priori for sin's continuity and existentiality.

2. Sin is understood as a pre-temporal deed underlying the sin of the present (of this view Julius Müller is the latest exponent); all speculative dualism tends to subscribe to this conception, as well as metaphysical theories of satanic revolt. Here an ontological *prius*, in the shape of an entity with all the fixity of " there is ", is given undialectical primacy over the act of sin.

Yet as entity sin cannot touch me existentially: I transcend it, I remain its master even when it overpowers me. Sin conceived as entity is man's exculpation. A mode of being must be ascribed to sin which on the one hand expresses its contingency, hence the complete inexculpability of the recurrent act, and on the other admits an interpretation of sin as the master of man to whom man has utterly delivered himself. The New Testament itself lays in our hands the very concept of being which we seek: Adam as I, and as the person of humanity.

In the judgment brought upon me by the death of Christ I see myself perish in my entirety; for I myself, the whole person, am guilty as the actor of my life, the taker of its decisions, which again and again were self-seeking: I determined myself in false ways, therefore Christ is my death, and because I wished to be alone the master, I am alone in my death. But Christ's death kills the whole of my humanity, kills humanity in the man; for I am I and humanity in one: in my fall from God, humanity fell. And so the I's debt before the Cross grows to monstrous dimensions; it is very Adam, the very first to do the inconceivable, he who does it still—sin, the act. But in this act, whose whole weight I continue to lay upon me as a charge with each sinful occasion, I find myself already in the humanity of Adam, or I see that in me, necessarily, humanity does also this my own free deed. As man the I is permanently consigned into this old humanity, which came to fall through me. As an individual it " is " not, for it is and was always in humanity. And for the very reason that the deed of the individual is also the deed of humanity, man must know himself responsible for the entire guilt of mankind. It is not possible to demonstrate the peculiar interrelation of individual and humanity as a causal connection—otherwise the " entity " mode would once more come into play—but knowledge of it is given to the individual as part of God's judgment, and it is knowledge of a kind which cannot be detached from the judgment and manipulated in theoretical abstraction for purposes of exoneration. On the contrary; because each person, as a human being, stands within the humanity of Adam, he may not sever himself from the sinful act and would not thereby rediscover a sinless being: the whole of his being, as a person, is in sin. Thus in Adam act is as constitutive for being as being for act; but both act and being come into judgment as laden with guilt. It is not in terms of historicalising theories, psychologising interpretations, that the structure of Adam's humanity should be conceived; rather should it be thus regarded: I myself am Adam, am I and humanity together; in me falls humanity; as I am Adam, so is every individual, but then in all individuals the one person of humanity, Adam, is active. This expresses both the contingency of the act and the continuity of being in sin. Because sin is envisaged in the concept of " Adam ", in the " person " mode of being, the contingency of conduct is preserved in the person of humanity, who I also am, and is combined with the continuity proper to the person, while conversely the person is attested—being act—by responsible conduct itself.

This conception is in general agreement with the definition of sin given by Luther—who wished it to be envisaged equally as original sin and as individual conduct and guilt —as self-seeking, as the individual person's seeking to possess himself. The being of sin has the personal mode. When I know of my being a sinner *qua* individual, I see that my *Dasein* is in the power of my *Wiesein* [1]: I cannot know it in its creatureliness. When I know of my being a sinner

[1] See p. 157, n. 1, above (*Translator*).

qua humanity, I see that my sinful *Dasein* is the basis of my *Wiesein;* yet I never see this as an exoneration, as if I occupied the position of a detached observer looking at a fixed entity: on the contrary, I see my existence within the frame of judgment, inasmuch as I know I must die as " Adam ".

c. *Everydayness, temptation and the knowledge of conscience*

The *everydayness* of man in Adam is guilt. It is the option for self-isolation, which is a decision constantly in process of being taken, because it has already been taken. It is the creature's wilful and compulsive quest for enjoyment, and as such it is constantly in flight from matters whose acknowledgment sets bounds to the business of enjoyment: death and oneself, as rightly known. But because flight is hopeless [1] (for if not to-day, then in death, man must stand exposed before the judgment-seat of Christ—II Cor. 5, 10), the everydayness of Adam is desperation—and that all the more, the wilder the flight and the less man is conscious of despair. Superficiality is the mask of lonely isolation; it is directed lifeward, but its beginning and end is death in guilt.

Conscience, as the becoming aware of despair and isolation, seeks to overcome them through this very awareness. Isolation is not grasped in its true sense; there arises merely a general consciousness of being left alone, and Adam proposes to correct this by conscience itself, by reducing himself to his own resources. In conscience the powers of the world, the law and death, loom large to threaten and frighten; life erupts into man's fear of himself, because he

---

[1] Cf. Luther, *Röm. Komm.*, Ficker 236, 31.

is ignorant of the future and has no control over its course. Yet there is also in this fear an inability to break free of oneself, a final lingering of the I on itself. In conscience death rises over the I's horizon, but only as an entity, as a phenomenon which may be forced to terms by conscience itself. Man knows himself immortal, and remains alone.

That this being-alone has the character of guilt is revealed through the *temptation* wherein Christ assails man through the law. Here all that went before grows to grim reality. Man is arrested in his ultimate flight, on the apparent escape-route of conscience, and he is forced to recognise that his guilt and death are the beginning and end of his flight. Moment by moment his guilt is bringing death down upon him; death is no longer an entity overcome; in the moment of recognising guilt and the curse of death, man sees that he is already in death; he is dead before he dies, and he is dying anew each moment.[1] Death is the very source of all his knowledge and volition, for they do not come from the life of God. This constant dying is accompanied with fear and woe. Guilt, death and the mundane press in upon man, making the world too "narrow"

[1] On this point cf. Heidegger's analysis of " being to death " as the " proper potentiality " realisable by the " entirety of existence ". Heidegger's concept of death is metaphysical and at bottom a false metaphor, since he includes death in the process of mind finding itself, i.e. " *Dasein* ". Inasmuch as " being to death " is not, for him, an ontic-existential experience but part of the ontological-existential structure of *Dasein*, death is incorporated in living existence. The Christian account is very different: in death, to which man in Adam has as such always forfeited himself, and into which he has always lapsed, existence finds its real end, its terminus, not its wholeness, completion, perfection; here " end " *qua* finish and " end " *qua* fulfilment are identifiable only in the metaphysical system. Death is eternal death, unless Christ wake man from the dead (Eph. 5, 14).

for him [1]; no longer is he alone, for now everything speaks to him—as his accuser—yet he remains in this condition alone and defenceless. In this temptation,[2] man dies " of " Christ, dies " of " the law, which is nevertheless of the spirit.[3] In the death of the sinner, however, predestination is fulfilled; for one, eternal death; for another, eternal life. Temptation itself belongs to man in Adam, and must lead to death. It brings with it again and again the terrors of eternal death. In it sin, guilt and the law darken the Cross and resurrection, and they tempt man to accept them as final. Whether Christ will give himself to the tempted man in grace and faith is always in the balance, therefore temptatiin should never be regarded as a dialectical point of transition on the road to faith.[4] No; it is the real end of the sinner, his death; that life should grow out of death is the free gift of God to his communion, free even for the

---

[1] Luther, W.A. 2, 685f.: " Like as a child is born in fear and peril out of the little dwelling of its mother's womb into the wide heaven and earth of this world, so man goes out of this life through the narrow gate of death; likewise, though heaven and world appear great and wide to us now we are in life, yet all is far narrower and smaller against the Heaven to come than is our mother's womb against the heaven we see . . . thus in dying one should take comfort against fear, and know that a great spaciousness and joy will be thereafter".

Translator's Note: At this point in the text Bonhoeffer remarks that *Enge* (" narrowness "), *Angst* (" fear ") and *bange* (" woeful ") are words with a common root—which is of course shared by many words of constriction, etc. Examples: O.E. *ange* (" painful "), *angr—anger; angle, ankle, anguish, angina, anxious* (with Latin, Greek and other antecedents).

[2] Or " assault ", the literal sense of *Anfechtung* (*Trans.*).

[3] On this point also Kohlbrügge writes with a rare profundity, op. cit.

[4] Holl is inclined to this error; see his *Luther*, pp. 67ff. and *passim*.

168

man who " is " in the communion, i.e. finds himself believing. God can allow man to die " of " the knowledge of his sin, and can lead him through this death into the communion of Christ. In this case he turns man's eyes away from man's self and gives him his direction (the pure intentionality of the *actus directus*) to Christ the Crucified and Risen, who is the defeat of temptation to death.

2

BEING IN CHRIST

A. *Definition of " being " in Christ*

" Seek thyself only in Christ and not in thyself, then wilt
thou find thyself eternally in him." [1] Here the man *in se
conversus* [2] is torn away from the attempt to remain alone
with himself and is turned towards Christ. Now he lives
only in the contemplation of Christ.[3] This is the gift of
faith, that man no longer looks on himself but on salvation
alone, which has come to him from without. He finds
himself in Christ because he is already in Christ from the
fact of seeking himself there. If, through man's self-
incapsulation, *Dasein* in Adam was in subjection to his
Wiesein,[4] the sight of Christ brings the loosening of the
bonds: *Dasein* becomes free, not as if it were able to stand

[1] Luther, W.A. 2, 690.
[2] Luther, W.A. 40, 1; 282, 21ff.: " *sed hic opportet Christum et con-
scientiam meam fieri unum corpus, ita ut in conspectu meo nihil maneat nisi
Christus crucifixus et resuscitatus. Si vero in me tantum intueor excluso Christo,
actum est de me. . . . ibi in me conversus et considerans qualis ego sim vel esse
debeam, item quid mihi faciundum sit, amitto ex oculis Christum, qui solus est
iustitia et vita mea*".
[3] Luther, W.A. 40, 1: 283, 2, on Gal. 2, 20: " that is, ' *non ego* ': *non
inspicio me*".
[4] See p. 157, n. 1, above (*Translator*).

over against *Wiesein* as independent being, but in the sense
of escaping from the I's domination into the lordship of
Christ, where for the first time in original freedom it recognises itself as the creature of God.

Only in Christ does man know himself as the creature of
God; in Adam he was at once creator and created.[1] If he
is to know himself as the creature of God, the old man
must have died and the new arisen, whose essence it is to
live in self-disregard, wholly in the contemplation of Christ.
He knows himself as one who lives in Christ in identity
with the old man who has passed through death—knows
himself as the creature of God. That the sinner also is a
creature, the sinner can say only as a believer. As known
by the sinner it remains an idea in untruth.

It would seem logical here to demand that the ontological
definition of the being of man as sinnerhood and being-in-
Christ should be underpinned by a general ontology of the
creature.[2] In such a case we would have allied ourselves
with Catholicism. Creaturehood simply is only " in faith ":
it is the existence of the believer, which is inseparable from
the ontic mode called faith; it " is " not in the fixed entity-
mode of " there is ", but in the very movement of being
in faith. Ontologically this means that God is at once the
basis of the creature's being and his master. Transcendentally it means that the existence of the creature is " amid

[1] The possibility of forming the *idea* of a creator-god, which naturally
obtains even *in statu corruptionis*, is another matter. It is an idea which
cannot be understood as a *reality* by the individual in that state, for the
very reason that he continually postulates himself as his own creator.

[2] We have already rejected, in another connection, the other possibility, of seeking a groundwork in the phenomenological interpretation
of the existentiality of existence.

and with reference to " transcendence. There is no onto-logical specification of the creature independently of the fact that God is the atoner and redeemer while man is the sinner and forgiven. In the Christian doctrine of being, all metaphysical ideas of eternity and time, being and becoming, living and dying, essence and appearance must be compatible with ontological concepts of sin and grace, or they must be entirely recast. Only from this viewpoint is it possible to define the being of sin, the being of grace, the being of revelation, as being with the character of a union of act and being: as personal being. However, in the idea of the creature the personal being of God and of revelation is expressed as lord and creator over my human personal being. Creatorhood, in this conception, is the more exhaustive definition.

If it is only in faith that I am able to know myself as God's creature, I know further that God has in creating me placed me in my entirety, both as I and as humanity, in the context of nature and history; I know therefore that these circumstances are in some way affected by creatureliness. But creature-faith is reluctant to claim that the " world " that has come to be its own, determined in its *Wiesein* by sin and death and with its *Dasein* [1] in subjection, is God's creation. Nevertheless, God is still the Lord even of this world, and, looking to the hope offered by the resurrection of the historical (*geschichtlich*) Christ and my life with him, to which is promised a new Heaven and earth, faith must believe that in spite of its falling-away the world is God's creation. It follows that any theory of being which sought to be applicable to " purely creaturely being " must needs

[1] See p. 157, n. 1, above (*Translator*).

become a definition of being outside the revelation in Christ, even though it is only in Christ that a full and proper faith in divine creation may evolve.

If we now have the ontological task of demarcating the being of the creature as postulated in the being of sinner and justified alike, we must seek our answer simultaneously in the structure of man's *Dasein* (whether enslaved by sin or emancipated by grace) and in the structure of his *Wie-Sein*, i.e. his ontic orientation, his " being-directed-at ". His ontological condition, his " *Da* " [1] can never be specified independently of his ontic mode, his *Wie*. No metaphysical deductions or distinctions—*existentia, essentia, ens*—no onto-logical-existential structures are capable of hunting down the " *Da* " of creaturehood. To be a creature means to exist (*Dasein*) through God and for God in faith, i.e. speci-fically under the impact of revelation. This utterly general definition itself suffices to show that in the concept of creaturehood the *Da* and the *Wie* belong indissolubly together.

Creaturely existence—*Dasein*—exists, is " *da* ", only in the being-directed towards revelation; conversely, the being-directed is an ontological peculiarity of this " *Da* " as such. This is to say that both *Da* and *Wie* are, inextric-ably, based together on revelation and only on revelation. Only in this context is one's understanding of the *Da* and *Wie* safeguarded from adulteration with categories alien to the case.

[1] *Translator's note:* Bonhoeffer says simply " *Das* ' *Da* ' ", but this has been rendered " ontological condition " in order to eliminate the " actual fact " connotation (=*das Dass*) of *Dasein* when it is contrasted with " essence " or used to affirm reality. " Condition " must be understood as " foundation-state ".

Likewise it is only in revelation that creaturehood can be defined *qua* personal being, inasmuch as it is the person whose existence has been affected, redirected or re-created by Christ. Thus all our ontological definitions are connected with the revelation in Christ; only the concretions of sinnerhood and the being of the just man answer the case before us. But these do not abolish the idea of the creature; no, it is preserved and expressed in the concretion of " existence through and for God ". Neither do they exclude the possibility of theologically rethinking such " creaturely " categories as individuality, being in history and nature, being and becoming, etc., but this possibility depends on the presupposition of an existence affected by revelation.

To object that categories of a generally metaphysical nature have been employed in the foregoing is to overlook the necessity of a certain formal " pre-comprehension " as a standpoint from which questions—even if wrong ones— can be framed, whose answer is subsequently returned by revelation together with a fundamental correction of the question.

And so the idea of creation provides no basis on which to raise our definition of man's being in Christ. There " is " only man in Adam or in Christ, in unbelief or faith, in the humanity of Adam or the communion of Christ; there " is " God alone as creator, God as atoner and redeemer. The being of all these, moreoever, is personal being. The world of entity is transcended by this personal being, which also bestows on it its character: it " is for " man in Adam his own subjected, " interpreted " world imbued with the curse of death; it " is for " man in Christ the world delivered from the I yet newly subjected to it by God in the expectation of the new creation (Rom. 8, 19ff.); finally, it is absolutely for God, its eternal master. Its being has no more general definition.

Being in Christ, being-directed to Christ, makes existence free; man exists for and through Christ; he believes because he looks on Christ. In defining this faith in terms of pure intentionality one must avoid on the one hand the desire to pinpoint the temporality of faith—as is attempted not only by the theology of consciousness but, in my opinion, also by H. M. Müller in our own time [1] —and on the other hand the desire to locate in the act of belief itself the reflection which discovers faith only in the reflected form of faith-wishfulness. That is the danger in Barth. Faith and " faith -wishfulness " lie together in the same act. Every act of faith is " wishful " in so far as it is a happening embedded in the psychic and there accessible to reflexion. But faith properly so called lies in the act's intention towards Christ, which is founded in being in the communion of Christ. A faith which grows doubtful of itself because it considers itself unworthy is a faith which stands in temptation. Faith *itself* knows that it is not faith *qua opus* which justifies, but Christ alone, and this it does not need to be

[1] See his *Erfahrung und Glaube bei Luther*, 1928. The " times of need and stress (*Not*) " when faith overcomes temptation are said to be plainly demonstrable, but where is our criterion for distinguishing such occasions from self-stimulated experiences? Is it perhaps to be found in some special intensity of " experience "? Has Müller really avoided falling into psychologism? Only two persons can be sure of the reality of faith as distinct from faith-wishfulness; one is the believer who being in faith no longer questions, the other is Christ.

told by a reflexion which in addition says something quite different, inasmuch as it questions faith and brings it into temptation. Though Barth has theological right on his side when he chides Schleiermacher for his "great confusion" of religion and grace,[1] he undermines his position by introducing reflexion into the act of faith, with the effect of casting doubt on faith itself, therefore indirectly on Christ. This is the penalty paid for inadequately distinguishing between knowing in faith and theological cognition. Furthermore, there is a danger here of inadvertently allowing that wishful faith truly grasps Christ, whereupon all such ominous words as enthusiasm, the lively sense or religous " experience ", piety, feeling, conversion of the will must perforce return to currency. It must be plainly said that within the communion of Christ faith takes shape in religion, that therefore religion is here called faith, that, as I look on Christ, I may and must say for my consolation " I believe " —only to add, of course, as I turn to look on myself, " help Thou my unbelief ". All praying, all searching for God in his Word, all clinging to his promise, all entreaty for his grace, all hoping in sight of the Cross, all this for reflexion is " religion ", " faith-wishfulness "; but in the communion of Christ, while it is still the work of man, it is God-given faith, faith willed by God, wherein by God's mercy he may really be found. If faith wished to question its own sufficiency it would already have lapsed from intentionality into temptation. Say rather, then, that it assures itself of its content, inasmuch as it holds fast to it, draws it to itself, dwelling thus with undivided attention in the contemplation of Christ, which is destroyed only by reflexion on the self.

[1] Barth, *Dogmatik*, I, § 18, pp. 301ff.

Act and Being

Being in Christ is being turned to Christ, and this is possible only through "being already" (as we have described above) in the communion of Christ. And so the transcendental and ontological theses are re-united.

This is no more than the formal definition, as we may call it, of being in Christ. But in its historical actuality this being is similarly determined by both past and future (see p. 119 above). It is from this point that we may begin to see clearly the concrete mode of being shared by being-directed to Christ and being within the communion.

B. *The past as determinant of being in Christ: Conscience*

"Whoever lacks conscience is Christ or the spirit of evil" (*Theologia deutsch*). Historical man has a conscience, not only in Adam (as a shield against the attack of God) but also in the Church of Christ. Conscience is only where there is sin. Since, however, man in Christ is no longer ruled by sin, conscience represents a determination by the past in Adam. Man has conscience from and in himself; it does not belong to the things yet "to come". It is the reflexion on oneself which is the farthest limit of Adam's penetration. Primarily it is not the voice of God but man's own voice. But if being in Christ is purely intentional, if it is being-directed upon Christ, reflexion on the self is obviously excluded. This is the problem of the Christian conscience.

A distinction must be made between two forms of conscience appropriate to man in Christ:

1. Conscience is interposed between Christ (the communion) and myself; it obscures my view of Christ, or shows him to me as my judge from the Cross, thus pointing

constantly to my sin. The law of the spirit has risen against
me. I hear only my accuser, see myself cast out, death and
Hell reach out to seize me. In reality this is temptation [1]
and rebellion against Christ, for it is mistrust of the grace
offered in Christ. In this temptation the man in the communion of Christ also stands in real danger of losing Christ,
unless Christ himself comes forward to kill man's conscience,
confess himself anew to man and restore his faith. But in
faith man once more finds himself already in the communion;
he knows that even temptation by sin and death is overcome
in faith for him who stands in the communion. The opinion
that such temptation is needed in order to come to faith
resembles Hegel's dialectic in making evil a necessary stage
on the road to good. This temptation belongs wholly to
the righteousness of the flesh, and this conscience is itself
defection from Christ.

2. The other form of conscience, of reflexion on the self,
is comprised within the intention towards Christ. Whoever
seeks himself in Christ sees himself always in sin, but now
this sin is no longer able to distract the attention from Christ
—indeed, it is rather the basis from which I, ἐν σαρκί, can
contemplate Christ with such singleness of mind. I see my
sin in the context of my having been forgiven by Christ.
" Thus thou mayst surely look on thy sins from out thy
conscience (!), for there sins are no more sins, there they
are overcome and swallowed up in Christ . . . if thou but
believest this, they no longer cause thee harm ".[2] Furthermore, repentance is no longer the final attempt to grasp

---

[1] Cf. the whole of Luther's " Sermon on readiness to die ", 1519,
W.A., 2, 685ff.
[2] Luther, W.A. 2, 690.

oneself, but repentance in the confidence of forgiveness[1]—
contritio passiva. This is the meaning of daily penance and
repentance. Not a self-losing to oneself, but a self-finding
in Christ. Admittedly, even the reflexion of repentance has
life ἐν σαρκί as its precondition, the sin of falling away from
intentionality towards Christ. If there were no sin, repentance would be thanksgiving. This final hindrance by sin
to the pure contemplation of Christ is overcome in faith,
which sees sin henceforth only in the context of forgiveness
by Christ within the communion. This faith remains
penitence, but as such reflexion has lost its power to disrupt
the steady intention towards Christ; even now, of course,
intentionality is upon occasion drawn into conflict, for it
still lacks the pure form of " being determined solely by the
future " (see " C " below).

In the presence of Christ, and in Christ, the self-reflexion of
sinful man is the death of man ἐν οαρκί, just as the self-
reflexion of man in Adam was the death of man in the spirit.
Because Christ died, and because we in baptism have shared
his death (Rom. 6), death is embedded in faith, the death
which the believer must daily die. Neither ascesis nor self-
steeling give him strength so to die, for these remain the
work of natural man, who cannot desire a Cross and a
death; he dies solely in faith. He does not give himself
death, but sees himself, in faith, given into death by Christ.
He sees himself drawn into the daily death-throes of the
flesh, the agony of the old man; in the power of faith he can
see Christ wrestling with death within him. He has faith
in the victory of Christ, yet he is body and soul in the grip

[1] Cf. Luther's " Sermon on the sacrament of penance ", W.A. 2, 713ff.

of death. The death of the old man is guilt, which delivers the future to the past in compensation for having forcibly deprived it of the new man. The man over whom Christ's future has triumphed in faith must with open eyes die daily the death of this past. The harder death attacks him, the mightier is the power of the past over man. Thus being in Christ, which is determined by the past in the form of the reflexion, within faith, of repentance and dying, stands on determination by the future of life and sanctity.

c. *The future as determinant of being in Christ: the Child*

" Future " signifies the determination of being by something yet to come: something " coming " from outside. There is genuine futurity only through Christ, only through the reality, newly created by him, of one's neighbour and the creation. The world estranged from Christ is I-confined: it is, that is to say, already the past. Life in this world is reflexion. The yet-to-come demands outright acceptance or rejection; reflexion is here abnegation. Christ, the absolute *futurus*, demands faith, demands a reflexionless orientation upon him.

In this, even the second stage of reflexion is superseded, i.e. not only self-reflexion outside Christ but the reflexion of the " Christian " conscience described above. While sin persists, Christian conscience persists. But in pure intention toward Christ there is no sin, and there is therefore no reflexion of faith-ful repentance. In his determination by the future, man is wholly detached from himself by contemplation of Christ. Yet it is not, of course, a matter of self-dissolution in mystical vision; I see Christ as " my

Lord and my God ": that, however, is no longer a reflexion on the I but is a manner of expressing the personality of the relationship which is preserved even in the attitude of pure intention.

Fides directa is the name which has been given by traditional Protestant dogmatics to the act of faith which, though taking place in the consciousness of the person, cannot be reflected in it.[1] It rests on the objectivity of the event of revelation in Word and sacrament; the cleaving to Christ has no need to be conscious of itself: it is in any case wholly taken up with the performance of the *actus directus*. Man is in Christ; on that account he sees neither his sin nor his death, for there is neither sin nor death in Christ; furthermore he sees neither himself nor his own faith. He sees only Christ, as his Lord and his God. Seeing Christ in Word and sacrament means seeing, in one and the same act, the risen Crucified *in* one's neighbour and in creation. Here alone is the revelation of that future which determines the present in faith. The future's determination of being in Christ recapitulates the dialectic of act and

[1] On this point cf. Franz Delitzsch, *Biblische Psychologie*, 1855, pp. 301ff. These concern the *actus directi* and *reflexi* of the life of grace. On page 306 we read: " This *actus directus* has *in itself* God's promise. The *actus reflexi* of divine certification, joyful assurance, sensational (*empfindlich*) seeing and tasting, are not of the essence of justificatory faith, but this *actus directus* is, as our forefathers would have said, the *forma fidei essentialis*". And on page 298: " The processes named and promised by the Word (*scil.* rebirth) also happen to us in the depth of unconsciousness, and it is only now and again that reflexes therefrom enter our consciousness." And on page 299: " If the fact of rebirth were an event in the sphere of our consciousness, how could there possibly be such variance and uncertainty among enlightened minds as to the difference of effect of the Word and the sacraments? " Here of course a theological should replace the psychological interpretation.

being. In faith the future is the present; but inasmuch as faith suspends itself before the future (knowing itself as the future's mode of being, but not as productive of it), man " is " in the future of Christ, i.e. never in actless being, never in beingless act.

Willingness to be determined by the future is the eschatological possibility of the child. The child sees itself, in all fear and wonderment, gripped by the onrush of things to come, therefore it can live only for the present, but the grown man, willing to be determined by the present, lapses into the past, into himself, into death and guilt. It is only out of the future that the present can be lived.

Here the child poses the problem of theology. *Actus directus* or *actus reflexus ?*—infant baptism or religiosity? The *actus directus* and infant baptism, as associated by old-Protestant dogmatics, the one being the act directed solely by and on Christ, the other a paradoxical event of revelation devoid of any response in reflexive consciousness, these together are the eschatological upbeat under which life is poised.[1] Both are properly inconceivable save in connection with the last things. Baptism is the man's summons to the child, one which may be understood only in an eschatological sense. Only the community of its members can speak of the meaning of infant baptism. The child is neighbour to the *eschata*. This too is inconceivable save by the faith which abolishes itself in the presence of revelation. Faith may know

---

[1] Cf. Hollaz, *Examen; Cap. de gratia regenerante:* " *habent infantes fidem non reflexam aut discursivam, sed directam et simplicem a Spiritu Sancto, cui malitiose non resistunt per baptismum accensam* ". See also Delitzsch, op. cit., p. 301, and cf. our immediately preceding footnote.

that baptism is the unbreakable Word of God and the eschatological foundation of its life.

Because baptism, while lying in the chronological past, is yet an eschatological event, the whole of my past life acquires point and continuity. It lies between eternity and eternity, founded by God's Word and " referring " onward to God's Word. Thus my past, like that of the Christian communion in general, is founded, determined and " directed " by the future, which is woken from it by the Spirit.

To speak of the *actus directus* which may never be captured by reflexion (not my own act by myself, not to mention any second observer), to speak of infant baptism, of a self-abolishing faith, all this may appear to open prospects wherein not all roads are barred to the eschatology of an apocatastasis.[1] Yet this very talk of apocatastasis may not be much more than the wishful regret of theology, when it must speak of faith and unbelief, of election and rejection.

In pure direction to Christ, *Dasein* and *Wiesein* [2] are restored to their proper relationship. The " *Da* " is released from oppression by the *Wie*, while conversely the *Wie* rediscovers itself in the divinely appointed " *Da* "; the echoless crying

---

[1] Luther himself, in *Röm. Komm.*, II, 227, says that the *actus directus* may lie hidden under the guise of blasphemies: " *cum tales blasphemie, quia sunt violenter a diabolo hominibus invitis extorte, aliquando gratiores sonent in aure Dei quam ipsum Alleluja vel quecunque laudis jubilatio* ". " Now there are many who have truly seized on Christ even though they do not feel that they have him, and these are none the less justified " (Pontoppidan, *Heller Glaubenspiegel*, 1726 and 1768, quoted by Delitzsch, op. cit., p. 307).

[2] See p. 157, n. 1, and p. 173, n. 1, above (*Translator*).

out from solitude into the solitude of self, the protest against all kinds of duress, has unexpectedly received an answer: gradually it is resolved into the still and prayerful converse of the child with the Father in the Word of Jesus Christ. In contemplation of Christ, the tormented knowledge [1] of the I's laceration finds the " joyful conscience ", [2] confidence and courage. The slave is unbound. He who has grown to the man in exile and wretchedness grows to be the child as he finds his home. Home is the communion of Christ, which is always " future ", the present " in faith ", because we are children of the future; always act, because being; always being, because act.

Here in faith becoming a reality,[3] there in vision perfected, this is the new creation of the new man of the future, who no longer looks back on himself but only away from himself to the revelation of God, to Christ; the man who is born out of the narrowness of the world into the breadth of Heaven, who becomes what he was or, it may be, never was: a creature of God—a child.

---

[1] *Wissen—scientia* (*Translator*).

[2] *Gewissen—conscientia* (*Translator*).

[3] *Translator's note: Schon hier im Glauben Ereignis werdende*—Involuntarily, perhaps, or it may be as an oblique Lutheran correction of Goethe's " *ewig Weibliches* ", Bonhoeffer's choice of words recalls the final Chorus Mysticus of *Faust, Part Two:* " *Alles Vergängliche ist nur ein Gleichnis; das Unzulängliche, hier wird's Ereignis* . . ." of which the literal sense is " Everything that can be bygone is only a likeness; the inadequate here grows into a full actuality. . . ." See also p. 168, n. 1, above.

INDEX

INDEX

1. *Biblical references*

Index

II. Names

Index

III. Subjects

189

Index

Index

191